The Stars

The Stars

Edgar Morin

Translated by Richard Howard
Foreword by Lorraine Mortimer

University of Minnesota Press
Minneapolis • London

The photographs in this book were selected from the illustrations in
The Stars: An Account of the Star-System in Motion Pictures, an earlier
edition of this translation published by Grove Press in 1960.

Originally published as *Les Stars*. Copyright 1972 Éditions du Seuil

English translation copyright 2005 Richard Howard

Published by the University of Minnesota Press
111 Third Avenue South, Suite 290
Minneapolis, MN 55401–2520
http://www.upress.umn.edu

Library of Congress Cataloging-in-Publication Data

Morin, Edgar.
   The stars / Edgar Morin ; translated by Richard Howard ; foreword by
Lorraine Mortimer.—1st University of Minnesota Press ed.
      p.   cm.
   Translated from French.
   Includes bibliographical references.
   ISBN 0-8166-4122-6 (hc : alk. paper)—ISBN 0-8166-4123-4 (pb : alk. paper)
1. Motion picture actors and actresses. I. Title.
   PN1998.2.M668 2005
   791.43'028'0922—dc22

                                                          2005004655

Printed in the United States of America on acid-free paper

The University of Minnesota is an equal-opportunity educator and employer.

12 11 10 09 08 07 06 05   10 9 8 7 6 5 4 3 2 1

Contents

Foreword

Lorraine Mortimer

A French "intellectual monument," actively involved in contemporary social and political debate, Edgar Morin has long been preoccupied by the mythology and magic that live on in our so-called rational modern societies. In *The Stars*, as in his earlier book *The Cinema, or The Imaginary Man*, he presents us with a human reality that nourishes itself on the imaginary, to the point of being semi-imaginary itself. For him, the phenomenon of the star—a Marilyn Monroe, a Brigitte Bardot, or a James Dean—is at the crossroads of what we call the "aesthetic," the "magical," and the "religious." As stars are both divine and mortal, idols and commercial products, Morin believes that examining them calls for a multidimensional approach, situating the phenomenon of stardom historically, economically, culturally, and politically, while never pretending to explain away the experience of beauty, pleasure, and even love that stars can elicit from within us.

Considering stars of French and Hollywood cinema, Morin wrote this book as a participant observer, "as an author who lives in the myths he is analyzing." Convinced of the perils of condescending to the phenomena we study, he sees it as a dangerous illusion to treat our attachment to stars as merely a vestige of childishness in a modern, essentially rational, civilization. In *The Stars*, as in *The Cinema, or*

The Imaginary Man, Morin sees himself dealing with both the sociology of the contemporary world and "fundamental anthropology." He believes that along with historical and cultural variations and differences there are deep commonalities, shared human experiences of living in the world. Stars are a specific product of capitalist civilization, yet they can provoke and satisfy profound anthropological needs.

Whereas more conventional sociology so often seems to reduce the complexity of what it analyzes, diminishing its force and banishing its magic, for Morin the charisma of stars, if we take the concept of charisma put forward by Max Weber, can be regarded as a "force that disregards economy." Stars can bear gifts of the body and spirit capable of transcending the boundaries of everyday routines and structures. When we speak of charisma, we are transported to the domain of the heroic, the extraordinary, the magical. And, unlike in life, in film charisma is not dissipated and routinized. Congealed in the emulsion, it is released by the projector to radiate again and again—for Morin, with all the ambiguity and power of the ancient double.

Linking film and everyday life, Morin suggests that all affective participation involves projections and identifications. In life, we transfer to others feelings and ideas that we naively attribute to them rather than to ourselves. The same kinds of projections and identifications are excited by film, with our psychic participation all the stronger when we are spectators, physically passive before the actors on the screen. We may live the spectacle in an almost mystical fashion, mentally integrating ourselves with the star characters while mentally integrating them within ourselves.

Stars also take part in their own rites, to which we have access. Each year at the Cannes Festival (as at the Academy Awards), they leave the screen and "offer themselves to mortal eyes. They condescend to have a body, a smile, an earthly gait, and even distribute the tangible proof of their incarnation: autographs." Cannes (like Hollywood) is the "mystic site" of an "identification of the magical and the real." In *The Cinema, or The Imaginary Man*, Morin cites early fantasy novels where stars, condemned to a life of parties and play, find their reality not in life but in a fake eternity, as shadows, ghosts. Acknowledging the "madness" involved in these rites and institutions, Morin nonetheless manages to analyze them without disenchanting them. Indeed, it is a premise of his work as a whole that, for better or worse, folly is an integral part of being human.

The chapter on James Dean is this book's crowning glory. Full-hearted, lyrical, and existentially sensitive, it well illustrates Morin's notion of the star as an "idea-force." *Rebel without a Cause* and *East of Eden* (both released in 1955) are conservative narratives. A beautiful boy wants his father's love. His mother has a touch of the monster about her. Overcoming emotional obstacles, the boy himself will probably mature into a good patriarch. Yet Dean seems to embody and express contradictions that deny the validity of the stereotypes we are asked to become in our everyday lives. He crosses barriers and explodes the categories the films put forward. His embodiment of vulnerability, his willingness to love and ask for love, questions the masculinity required in men's life scripts. Morin sees Dean as a mythological hero, expressing in his life and films the needs of adolescent individuality, refusing to accept the norms of the "soul-killing and specialized life that lies ahead." Dean's "adolescent" demand for "total life" is the antithesis of the resignation of the adult of our middle-class, bureaucratized society, "the man who agrees to live only a little in order not to die a great deal."

When Morin wrote *The Stars* in 1957, he was mindful of the transformation of stars and the cinema after the introduction of sound. Where the cinema audience had originally been more popular, juvenile, and appreciative of mass spectacle, he saw an evolution toward psychology and "realism," toward an increasingly middle-class cinematic imagination, with the mass of people aspiring to individuality, soul, romance, and love. The 1972 French edition of the book signaled changes occurring. Morin saw cinema branching into spectacular-escapist major productions and smaller, independent, "problem" films.[1] The French New Wave, launched in the late 1950s, had an impact worldwide. So too did cinema verité, born in 1960 as a result of Morin's own collaboration with ethnographic filmmaker and anthropologist Jean Rouch in the landmark documentary *Chronicle of a Summer*. Yet in 1957 he had already said that he was only suggesting preliminary steps for a general typology of stars, knowing their evolution to be manifold, complex, and varied, depending on countries of origin, and wondering, given the global dominance of Hollywood, about its effects on different national cultures, asking what innovations might be possible, what new syncretisms might eventuate.[2]

One might hope in these times of new and old barbarisms that scholars will feel the need to surrender some of their rationalist delusions, to lose, if they want to understand, the condescension they have so often shown to the "trivial" and "irrational" pleasures and passions of people around the globe. But too often the significance of what is important to people is belittled at the same time it is regretted. In *The Stars*, Morin includes a nice warning about this:

> Nonsense, no doubt! Nonsense from which the serious
> sociologist turns away in disgust. . . . But our scholars
> betray their frivolity in their refusal to take nonsense
> seriously. Nonsense is *also* what is most profound in man.
> Behind the star system there is not only the "stupidity"
> of fanatics, the lack of invention of screenwriters, the
> commercial chicanery of producers. There is the world's
> heart and there is love, another kind of nonsense, another
> profound humanity.

The Stars

Genesis and Metamorphosis of the Stars

The savage worships idols of wood and stone;
the civilized man, idols of flesh and blood.

—*George Bernard Shaw*

Throughout an immense part of the world, for an over-whelming proportion of the film industry, the movies revolve around a kind of solar performer appropriately called a *star*. The names and faces of the stars devour all movie advertisements; the name of the film itself scarcely counts. The director emerges from anonymity only exceptionally. "A film *with* Fernandel," we say, or "Garbo's last film": the stars rightly determine the very existence and economy of the movies. Scenarios are made to order for them.

A star can also transform a scenario already accepted by a studio: Marcel Achard and Marc Allégret must bow to the requirements of a star like Charles Boyer for a film that finally becomes *Orage*. A star can even impose a film's subject, as did Jean Gabin with *Escape from Yesterday*, *Pépé le Moko*, and *The Good Crew*, which Duvivier or Carné would perhaps not have succeeded in making without his intervention. There even comes a moment in his career at which a star selects the other stars to appear in his picture, his director, his writer, and so on, and becomes his own producer, like Eddie Constantine.

1

Certain directors are free to choose their stars: they are practically never free *not* to choose stars. Whether in films determined by the star or in films of which the star determines only the success, the star plays an essential role, at least in the capitalist atmosphere of the film world. The star can rescue a failing producer: in 1938–39 Deanna Durbin's box office set Universal Pictures on its feet again. Threatened by television after 1948, Hollywood sought and found its salvation not only in the panoramic screen but in superstars like Marilyn Monroe as well.

Furthermore, in the composition of the unpredictable alloy that constitutes a film, the star is the most precious and therefore the costliest substance. David O. Selznick, deciding to make *Gone with the Wind*, realized not only that Clark Gable was appropriate for the character of Rhett Butler, but that the character of Rhett Butler had been modeled after Clark Gable. He was forced to sign a leonine contract with Metro-Goldwyn-Mayer in order to obtain Clark Gable's services; Leo Rosten estimates that MGM's profits were as high as those of Mr. Selznick.

Fabulous sums distinguish the paychecks of the stars from those of ordinary actors. Martine Carol, Michèle Morgan, or Brigitte Bardot will today cost a film, of which the budget is estimated between 100 and 200 million francs, 20 to 40 million francs. The incomes of Hollywood's great stars exceed those of the most important producers.

The star system extends beyond the screen: five hundred correspondents are assigned to Hollywood to feed the world news and gossip about the stars. Margaret Thorp, in *America at the Movies*, estimates that one hundred thousand words are sent from Hollywood every day, making it America's third largest source of information, after Washington and New York.

Movie stars rule over radio and television alike. In 1937 they appeared on or endorsed 90 percent of major American radio programs. The stars endorse everything: toilet

Heidi Would
Love To Meet
You on Page 4

Daily Mirror

FINAL
EDITION 4c

NEW YORK 17, N. Y., FRIDAY, JANUARY 15, 1954

MARILYN, JOE WED

• Story on Page 3 •

New Mr. and Mrs., baseball great Joe DiMaggio and glamorous Marilyn Monroe blissfully embrace after San Francisco ceremony.

articles, makeup, refrigerators, beauty contests, racing competitions, athletic events, six-day bicycle races, benefits for writers at war or for noncombatant writers, charity bazaars, election campaigns. Their photographs are front-page material in newspapers and magazines. Their private life is public; their public life, publicity. The stars play a social and moral role as well; they satisfy the gossip columns of the heart. One producer even had the notion of consoling Sacco's wife at the moment of her martyred husband's execution by the presence of Bette Davis (who declined to figure in this exhibition). The star participates in all the world's joys, pities all its misfortunes, intervenes constantly in its destiny.

A stage actor has never become a star to this degree, has never been able to play so important a role within and beyond the spectacle. The movies have invented and revealed the star. Which is a curious paradox: the star seems to exist at the solar center of the movies, and yet the star system was grafted to the production system of the movies only after fifteen years of anonymous evolution. The original phenomenon of the star has nothing originating and apparently nothing necessary about it: nothing in the technical and aesthetic nature of the movies immediately required the star. On the contrary, the movies can ignore the actor, the quality of his work, even his presence, and replace him advantageously by amateurs, children, objects, or animated cartoons. And yet, capable as it is of forgoing the actor, the cinema invents or hypostatizes the star when the star in no way seems to participate in its essence. The stars are typically a cinematic phenomenon, and yet there is nothing specifically cinematic about them. It is this unspecific specificity that we must, if possible, explain and, first of all, describe.

Shortly after its birth, the cinema dreamed of calling on the services of the established stars of the theater. May Irvin and John Rice joined their lips together in Raff and Gammon's

Kiss. Sarah Bernhardt and the actors of the Comédie-Française contributed performances to art films. But the era of theater stars, in theater roles and theater decors, was ephemeral.

The star develops along with the new heroes of the movies, interpreted by anonymous and impecunious actors. The characters of the serial shorts—Nick Carter, Fantomas—pierce beyond the screen: suddenly, from the four corners of the world, arrive the first love letters addressed to Nick Carter. But Nick Carter is not a star; he is a film hero. The name of his interpreter, Liebel, is unknown.

Analogously, the comic heroes, spontaneously baptized Max, then Fatty, Picratt, and so on, by the public, herald the appearance of the stars. Already the interpreter, although still anonymous, makes his requirements felt. Max Linder, engaged in 1905 by Pathé for a fee of 20 francs, by 1909 received 150,000 francs a year. The decisive stage approaches when the personality of the interpreter breaks from the character he is playing as if from a chrysalis; the character will also have to be diversified, and the unique hero of the series makes way for multiple heroes, different but at the same time alike, according to the requirements of the film. Then the interpreter's name becomes as important as, and even more important than, that of the character he plays; and finally the dialectic of the actor and the role is instituted, a machine in which the star descends upon the earth. The movies, in fact, metamorphose themselves under the pressure of an increasingly insistent force: the role of love swells and sweeps the screen; the female countenance rises to its zenith in the movies.

The star ferments within the hero and the heroine. Zukor, realizing that the public wants stars, returned to Sarah Bernhardt, bought the French "art films," and founded the Famous Players (1912–13). The Famous Players were not to be the old principals of the stage, but new and adorable faces: Carl Laemmle snatches Mary Pickford from Biograph and offers her a contract at $195. The producers, who have preferred to plant their own names or those of their companies in the public awareness, from now on promote the stars. The era of the "Star Film" is over; that of the film stars, beginning.

These new stars spring from their characters as heroes or heroines. Originally determined by their roles, the stars determine them in their turn: after 1914 Tebo Mari refuses to wear a beard as Attila, and for the same reasons Alberto Capozzi rejects the role of St. Paul: the first stars declare themselves.

From 1913–14 to 1919 the star is crystallized both in the United States and in Europe. Mary Pickford, little Mary, is the first and the exemplary star: her nickname, "America's Sweetheart," offers her to the projection-identification of every spectator. At the same time appear the Italian diva (Francesca Bertini, melodramatic and love possessed) and the Danish vamp, who—imported to the United States with Theda Bara—introduces the direct kiss on the lips: no longer Raff and Gammon's stage kiss, but the prolonged union in which the ghoul sucks up her lover's soul. Shortly after 1918, Cecil B. DeMille launches the piquant, exciting girl who will prescribe for all Hollywood the new canons of "beauty-youth-sex-appeal."

Simultaneously the first male stars appear—not yet "love idols," but heirs of the marvelous heroes of the early shorts, acrobatic and hard-fisted athletes. They triumphantly establish their names by the supple strength of their knees, like Douglas Fairbanks, or by valorous cross-country cavalcades, like Tom Mix.

By 1919 the content, production, and publicity of the movies are focused on the star. The *star system* is henceforth at the center of the film industry. Then begins, from 1920 to 1931–32, a glorious era. Several great archetypes polarize the screen. The innocent or roguish virgin with immense, credulous eyes and half-open or sweetly mocking lips (Mary Pickford, Lillian Gish in the United States; Suzanne Grandais in France). The vamp of the North and the great prostitute of the Mediterranean reveal their separate essences and sometimes blend into the great archetype of the femme fatale, who rapidly becomes universal: in 1922, Shoharo Hanayagi introduces the vamp into the Japanese cinema.

Between the virgin and the femme fatale blossoms *la divine*, as mysterious and as sovereign as the femme fatale, as profoundly pure and as destined to suffer as the young virgin. *La divine* suffers and causes suffering. Garbo incarnates "the beauty of suffering," says Balázs. "It is the suffering of solitude. . . . Her pensive gaze comes from far away."[1] She is elsewhere, lost in her dream, inaccessible. This is the source of her divine mystery. The schizophrenic idol is opposed to the ever-present woman, companion or sister, who does not inspire adoration—that is, love. She transcends the femme fatale by her purity of soul.

The great masculine archetypes also make their appearance. The comic hero stars in a full-length film. Around the heroes of justice, adventure, and daredevil feats—cinematic progeny of Theseus, Hercules, Lancelot—crystallize the great epic genres.

To the hero of the adventure story is added the hero of the love affair, "*l'homme fatale*," with his feminized features and fiery glance. From these two archetypes Rudolph Valentino fashions a perfect synthesis: the Arab sheik, the Roman lord, the aviator; the god who dies, is reborn, and undergoes metamorphosis, Osiris, Attys, Dionysus—hero of innumerable exploits, he remains above all the "idol" of love.

To their apogee on the screen corresponds the apogee of the mythico-real life of Hollywood's stars. Sublime, eccentric, they build themselves pseudofeudal chateaus, houses copied from antique temples, with marble swimming pools,

menageries, private railroads. They live at a distance, far beyond all mortals. They consume their lives in caprice. They love each other, destroy each other, and their confused passions are as fatal in life as in the movies. They are unaware of marriage except to princes and aristocrats. Pola Negri gives her hand to Count Eugene Domski, then to Prince Serge Mdivani. Fanatic adoration surrounds them. The death of Rudolph Valentino is the culminating point of the stars' great epoch: two women commit suicide in front of the hospital where Valentino has just died; his funeral rolls by in an atmosphere of collective hysteria; his grave is still covered with flowers.

Garbo, in our midst and yet not among us, bears witness today to the star's former greatness. Too big for a cinema that had grown too small, she hardly deigned to make a few last films before shutting herself up in definitive silence. A survivor of the twilight of the gods, her mystery and her solitude permit us to measure the evolution that has taken place. As if as a sign of mourning, as though to protect herself from the corruptions of the world and time alike, she hides her features beneath graceless hats and impenetrable dark glasses. And it is her immortal, divine face that our memory sees gleaming beneath her veil.

After about 1930, the cinema, which is transforming itself, begins to transform the stars. Movies become more complex, more "realistic," more "psychological," and more cheerful. The great cinematic genres—fantasy, romance, adventure, crime, comedy, and so on—have already, of course, begun to enrich each other by reciprocal transfusions; certain themes (love, for instance) are diffused throughout every category of film; furthermore, each genre tends more or less to integrate as a minor theme what might be the keystone of another genre. In other words, a natural and progressive evolution tends to assemble at the heart of each film what had originally flourished in specialized genres.

This evolution is related, as we shall see, to the evolution and the enlargement of the moviegoing public. It is stimulated by research for a maximum profit: the multiplication of themes (romantic, adventurous, comic) at the heart of the same film attempts to respond to the greatest possible number of individual demands, that is, addresses itself to a potentially total public. The rise in the initial cost of filmmaking, due to technical improvements and the integration of the sound system, and the reduction of the public after the Crash of 1929 effect their almost simultaneous stimulations in the direction of this thematic complexity.

Furthermore, the "talkies" upset the equilibrium of real and unreal that the silent film had established. The concrete truth of sounds, the precision and nuances of words, if they are in part counterbalanced, as we will indicate below, by the "magic" of voices, songs, and music, nevertheless determine a "realistic" climate. Hence, moreover, the scorn of scenario writers for the new invention that, in their eyes, disenchanted the film.

In other respects Hollywood proceeds in a mood of optimism in order to permit its public to forget the effects of the "Great Depression." The *happy ending* becomes a requirement, a dogma. Most films are tinted with an agreeable fantasy, and a new genre, the bright comedy, is enthroned after Frank Capra's *It Happened One Night*. New optimistic structures promote the spectator's "escape" and thus in one sense avoid realism. But in another, the mythic content of the movies is "secularized," brought down to earth.

Finally, already subject to the influence of the Crash (King Vidor's *Our Daily Bread*) and subsequently to the progressive currents of the New Deal, the American cinema receives the full effect of social themes in all their realistic vitality (*Fury, Mr. Deeds Goes to Town, The Grapes of Wrath*).

All these factors determine the evolution of the film. But this evolution itself is controlled by a still deeper current, which is the increasingly middle-class nature of the cinematic imagination. Originally a mass spectacle, the movies had taken over the themes of the popular serial story and the melodrama, which provided, in an almost fantastic state, the first archetypes of the imaginary: providential encounters, the magic of the double (twins, speaking likenesses), extraordinary adventures, oedipal conflicts with stepfather or stepmother, orphans of unknown parenthood, persecuted innocence, and the hero's sacrificial death. Realism, psychological awareness, the happy ending, and humor reveal precisely the extent of the middle-class transformation of this version of the imaginary.

The projection-identifications that characterize the personality at the middle-class level tend to identify the imaginary and the real and to feed on each other. The middle-class version of the imaginary draws closer to the real by multiplying the signs of verisimilitude and credibility. It attenuates or undermines the melodramatic structures in order to replace them with plots that make every effort to be plausible. Hence what is called "realism." The resources of realism include fewer and fewer coincidences, "possession" of the hero by an occult force, and comprise more and more "psychological" motivations. And the same impulse that draws the imaginary to the real identifies the real with the imaginary. In other words, the soul's life broadens, enriches itself, even hypertrophies at the heart of middle-class individuality. For the soul is precisely that symbiotic *site* where real and imaginary encounter and feed on each other; love, that phenomenon of the soul that mingles most intimately our imaginary projection-identifications and our real life, assumes an increased importance.

It is within this framework that the middle-class concept of romance develops. The imaginary is affected much more directly by the real, and the real much more intimately by the imaginary: the affective relation between spectator and hero becomes so personal, in the most egoistic sense of the word, that the spectator now retreats from what he had

previously required—the hero's death. The happy ending substitutes for the tragic finale. Death and destiny recoil before a providential optimism.

Realistic, psychological, optimistic lines of force determine the evolution of the movies in a particularly apparent way after 1930. This indicates that the film is progressively enlarging its public, originally popular and juvenile, in order to reach every age and every level of society. It means too that after 1930 there is an acceleration in the movement of the great mass of people to the psychological level of middle-class individuality. This revolutionary accession is a key phenomenon of the twentieth century, and it must be considered as a total human phenomenon, for it also develops on the political and social level; on the level of everyday affective life it is expressed by new affirmations of and new participations in individuality.

The affective life is, as we have said, both imaginary and practical. Men and women of rising social groups no longer caress only disembodied dreams: they tend to live their dreams as intensely, as precisely, and as concretely as possible; they even assimilate them into their lovemaking. They accede to the soul-civilization of the middle class, that is, Bovaryism.

The amelioration of material conditions of existence, a certain social progress, no matter how fragile (vacations with pay, shortening of the workday), new needs and new leisure make increasingly urgent one fundamental demand: the desire to live one's own life—that is, to live one's own dreams and to dream one's life.

A natural movement impels the great mass of people to accede to the affective level of the middle-class personality: their needs are modeled on the ruling standards of authority, which are those of middle-class culture. These needs are stimulated and channeled by the means of communication that are the property of the middle class. Thus the increasingly middle-class nature of the cinematic version of the imaginary corresponds to the increasingly middle-class nature of the psychology of the great mass of people.

The stars comply with this evolution all the more precisely since the requirements of affective assimilation are essentially addressed to the heroes of the cinema. Of course these heroes remain heroes—that is, models and mediators—but, by combining the exceptional and the ordinary, the ideal and the everyday, ever more intimately and diversely permit their public to identify itself with them by means of certain increasingly realistic points of reference.

In 1931 James Cagney hit Mae Clarke in the eye with a grapefruit. This gesture and this ignoble projectile were to unleash myriad "lower-class" gestures, soon followed by ludicrous gestures, flabbergasted faces, and all kinds of social blunders (bright comedies). The trivial and the comic are at last compatible with the star, who is no longer a marble idol. Even the star's face will respond to the "realistic" norms of makeup. (The quotation marks are necessary to remind us that even the most "realistic" makeup transfigures the reality of the face.) The special makeup of silent movies "concealed the physiognomy beneath masks of fantastic beauty, but the realism of the modern film has changed all that. The art of today's makeup artist consists in avoiding all artifice."[2] Pushed to its limit, realism tends to eliminate the star altogether (the neorealist Italian movies). But this limit is rarely attained, precisely because the film remains within the framework of the middle-class version of the imaginary. The example of the happy ending is significant: the spectator who prefers the comforting advantages of success (predominance of identification) to the purifying advantages of the hero's death (predominance of projection) is actually fostering a latent myth of immortality—the film ends with an ecstatic kiss—and time is henceforth immobilized, wrapped in cellophane. This optimism of the happy ending dissimulates, in fact, a greater fear of death than that shown in the lower-class version of the imaginary (in which the hero dies). The aggravation of this fear characterizes the middle-class conscience; it is expressed, in the framework of realism, by a flight from reality. Yet this artificial immortality, if it fosters the new star's mythic prestige, does not confer a privilege enjoyed by the stars of the great epoch, the prerogative of dying. Before 1930 the star was not afraid to steep himself in death. Immortality is the sign of a new fragility of the star-goddess.

The star-goddesses thus tend to "secularize" themselves to a certain degree, yet without losing their elementary mythic qualities. In the same manner and for the same reasons the great archetypes of the movies give way to a multitude of hero-gods of "average" greatness.

The concept of youth and beauty that fixed the ideal age of female stars between twenty and twenty-five, and that of male stars between twenty-five and thirty, has become more elastic. After 1930 we have the aging heroes of the middle-class theater in France (Victor Francen, Jean Murat), and after 1940, in Hollywood, the Clark Gables, Gary Coopers, Humphrey Bogarts, and so on, begin new careers as "the men who have really lived." The Max-Factorized heroine may actually reach forty. At the other end of the scale appear the adolescents: the stars henceforth endure for a longer age span and attain a larger physiognomic range as well: beauties are no longer always ideal, and even an interesting homeliness is permitted to impose its particular charm.

The former archetypes lose caste and give way to many subarchetypes that are more faithful to actual types. They do not altogether disappear; there is a continuous rebirth, within the new "realistic" framework, of the innocent virgin (Michèle Morgan in *Heart of Paris*, Etchika Choureau in *Les enfants de l'amour*), of the tragic hero who dies (Jean Gabin in *Port of Shadows*). But at the same time and progressively, the innocent virgin, the roguish little sweetheart, becomes the good sport, the feminine-masculine girl, both sweetheart and buddy, lover and friend.

To this decadence of the virgin corresponds the much more pronounced decadence of the vamp. The vamp, semi-fantastic in her destructive frigidity, can no longer adapt herself to the new realistic climate without absurdity. She immediately becomes a minor character, and a ridiculous one as well: her long cigarette holder and her fatal glance are material for comedy. The vamp stars change their roles; Marlene Dietrich humanizes herself and places her eroticism at the service of her big heart.

Similarly, the pure, desexualized hero of Wild West justice is eroticized and yields to his amorous weaknesses. In his own way, he too humanizes himself. The acrobatic hero becomes an enthusiast of outdoor sports, no longer an archangel overwhelming demons, but a well-built brawler. The furious Achilles, Theseus, and Hercules are from now on tough boys (James Cagney, Alan Ladd) who can prove only by the way they handle a pistol their ancient and marvelous infallibility. All have hearts ready for love. Reciprocally, the effeminate young romantic leads discover a new manly playfulness. The infantile and desexualized comedy hero has more and more claim to seduce his heroine: virility is etched on the timid features of even the most simple-minded clown.

These decompositions and combinations of types are nevertheless dominated by the flowering, since 1940, of two synthetic archetypes that have tended to renew the stars' luster. The former vamp, in disintegrating, liberated an erotic energy to be diffused among every type of star. The knowing good sport, the nightclub singer or showgirl, already appropriates a part of the vamp's sex appeal. Similarly, the ex-vamp herself becomes a good sport beneath her provocative exterior. But a kind of synthesis of vamp, sweetheart, and virgin functions in the realm of *glamour* to produce the *good-bad girl*. The good-bad girl's sex appeal rivals that of the vamp in that she appears in the guise of an impure woman: scanty clothes, bold attitudes, and provocative double entendres, an equivocal metier, suspect acquaintances. But the end of the film reveals she was merely hiding all her virginal virtues: purity of soul, natural goodness, and a generous heart.

In the same way, the *good-bad boy* represents the synthesis of the former brute beast and the arbiter of justice. William Powell, Wallace Beery, Humphrey Bogart, ex-debauchees,

become virile heroes, equivocal of course, but profoundly human. Inversely, the oversweet or timid ex-young romantic leads develop bad manners. Clark Gable becomes the sarcastic Rhett Butler of *Gone with the Wind*, Gary Cooper the blasé adventurer of *Blowing Wild*, Robert Taylor the fierce Roman centurion of *Quo Vadis*, but within this cynical and brutal envelope they preserve an exquisite soul.

Humphrey Bogart, in *The Maltese Falcon* (1941), incarnates the new synthesis that the crime film (film noir) is to spread over the whole American screen. The crime film suppresses the opposition of the odious ex-gangster and the good policeman–arbiter of justice, proposing instead a new, confused, and confusing type: the private eye of the novels of the great Dashiell Hammett, the all-too-human outlaws of the stories of R. Burnett or Henderson Clark. Half good, half bad, these good-bad boys can ignore the happy ending (reserved only for the virtuous) and occasionally revive the tragic hero of the old mythologies (Jack Palance in *Sudden Fear*; Jean Servais in *Rififi*).

The new synthesis of *bad* and *good* gives rise to great new screen idols, reanimating the divine qualities of the star even in the flood tide of his secularization. The immense erotic energy that floods the screen today is liberated in the chemical encounter of *good* and *bad*, simultaneous with the crystallization of the new *good-bad* complex.

Eroticism is the sexual attraction that spreads to all parts

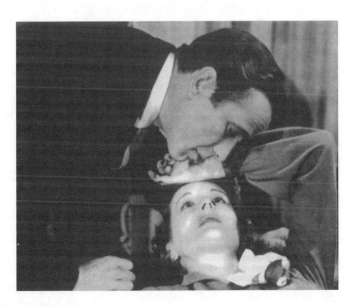

of the human body, fixing itself notably upon faces, clothes, and so on. It is also the imaginary "mystique" covering the whole domain of sexuality. The new stars are all eroticized, whereas formerly the virgin and the arbiter of justice partook of the purity of Mary or Lohengrin, and the vamp and the villain focused on themselves the bestial or destructive summons of sexuality.

The evolution is thus a general one: a greater degree of eroticization, "realistic" humanization, new typological combinations of the stars. We must nevertheless note a remarkable backwash provoked by the sound film. The sound film, by the same impulse that determines a new realism, gives rise to a new magic: song. Hence we see vocal stars like Bing Crosby and Luis Mariano make their appearance, rising to box-office peaks. Their syrupy voices are the equivalent of the sweet type of beauty of the young romantic leads of the silent screen. Heroes of musical films or operettas, these crooners excite a prepubertal and female idolatry that recalls the great cults of the silent films.

With this notable exception, the star system seemed fixed in its new orbit during the years after World War II, and perhaps, in a sense, even gave a few slight signs of being winded: the star's royal omnipotence seemed to be changing into a constitutional monarchy; the quality of the films and the names of the directors assumed a progressively greater importance in the eyes of a vastly increased public. A few films triumphantly managed to do without stars; but the integrity of the star system was not really questioned.

It was in these circumstances that in 1947 a serious box-office crisis affected the United States, England, France, and the Benelux nations. Although it has in no way provoked this crisis, the development of television has aggravated it, and it is first of all in its struggle with television that the movies have sought a means of surmounting the crisis. The screen is enlarged and color is imposed there definitively.

But the cinema also seeks and finds salvation in exoticism

and in history. Ancient Rome, the Knights of the Round Table, provide their mythic glamour, although always at the heart of credibility: history and geography are tests of truth and at the same time sources of the marvelous. The cinema does not escape into the fantastic, but into time and space and CinemaScope and Technicolor. Simultaneous with the new exoticism and history, a return to adventure and violence (the hero) and to eroticism (the heroine) has had the effect of regilding the star's prestige.

The erotic recovery plays a capital role: the mammary renaissance indicates the renaissance of the star system itself. "Lollobrigidism" lowers décolletés further than ever, revealing the stereoscopic charms of Gina, Sophia, and Martine. The movies multiply scenes of the stars stripteasing, swimming, undressing, dressing again, and so on. A tidal wave of perverse innocence bears erotic gamines like Audrey Hepburn, Leslie Caron, Françoise Arnoul, Marina Vlady, and Brigitte Bardot toward fame.

Brigitte Bardot's reputation is especially remarkable in that it virtually antedated the release of her films. Introduced at the Cannes Festival three years ago, she was immediately snatched up by the star-making machine because of her admirable qualities of extreme innocence and extreme eroticism. She was, with a vengeance, "the sexiest of the baby stars, and the babiest of the sexy stars."

Actually, her kittenlike face simultaneously expresses the infantile and the feline: the long hair falling down her back is the very symbol of lascivious undress, the proffered nudity, yet a deceptively disordered row of bangs across her forehead reminds us of the little high school girl. Her tiny roguish nose accentuates both her *gaminerie* and her animality; her fleshy lower lip is pursed into a baby's pout as often as into a provocation to be kissed. The little cleft in her chin adds the final touch to the charming *gaminerie* of this face, of which it would be libelous to say it has only one expression—it has two: eroticism and childishness.

The cinema has determined her nature with great exactitude and appropriateness: a little creature on the frontiers of childhood, of rape, of "nymphomania," all of whose roles necessarily revolve around a central striptease: in *The Light across the Street*, she swims naked in the river; in *Les week-end de Nero* (in which Brigitte Bardot plays Poppaea), "her bath in mare's milk is one of the film's chief attractions"; in *En effeuillant la Marguerite*, Agnès-B.B. enters a striptease contest; in *And God Created Woman*, the striptease reaches its paroxysm and is even accompanied by "the year's most sensual mambo." As *Cinémonde* puts it, "Shuddering with sensuality, Brigitte lets herself be enchanted by the music and the dance, enchanting creature that she is, undulating, quivering, swaying her hips with intentional lewdness to the rhythm of the most erotic of modern dances."

Hollywood goes still further. Not only does it launch new stars by means of a coarse swing of the hips or an aggressive bust, it creates a new love idol (Ava Gardner), when required, with a dash of vampirism. Marilyn Monroe, the torrid vamp of *Niagara*, naked under her red dress, with her ferocious sexuality and her sulky face, is the perfect symbol of the star system's recovery.

But her post-Niagaran career demonstrates that the dead vamp cannot be resuscitated: the Monroean vampirism must necessarily dissolve into the *good-bad girl*. Thus in *River of No Return* Marilyn Monroe metamorphoses into a nightclub singer with a big heart: we recognize her from the first scenes, an idol of lust singing the praises of the silver dollar with the voice of love, the model foster mother of a little orphan boy. Marilyn (if the reader will allow this familiarity to an author who lives in the myths he is analyzing) completely adapts herself to the star norms of 1930 with *How to Marry a Millionaire* and *The Seven Year Itch*. She accepts secularization of bright comedy by becoming a nearsighted blonde in search of a husband or a local beauty out to make her fortune in New York. Today she envisages major roles heavy with soul significance, reads Dostoyevsky, muses over Shakespeare, makes movies with Sir Laurence Olivier, and marries Arthur Miller. It is appropriate to the stellar order that a superstar marry a genius.

Thus, without ceasing to produce all her disturbing manifestations, the ex-vamp has arrived at the summit of spirituality. Marilyn's example is significant. The star system seems to be ruled by a thermostat: if the humanizing tendency that reduces the star to the human scale brushes everyday life a little too closely, an internal mechanism re-establishes her distance, a new artifice exalts her, she recovers altitude. Yet every excess in this direction provokes a recall to "realism." In other words, the evolution that has taken place since 1930 is irreversible, although it still cannot cross the decisive boundary on the other side of which the whole star system would totter. The star system hedge-hops rather than soars above our daily life.

This evolution from 1930 to the present affects the star's real life as well as her cinematic image. The star has actually become familiar and familial. Before 1930 she ignored middle-class marriage and was connected only with stars of the same magnitude. Subsequently, she was permitted to marry minor actors, businessmen, doctors. She no longer lives in a pseudofeudal chateau, or a pseudo-Greek temple, but in an apartment, a townhouse, even a ranch. She exhibits in all simplicity the life of middle-class comforts: she knots a flirtatious apron around her hips, turns on the stove, and cooks ham and eggs. Before 1930 the star could not be pregnant; today she is a mother and an exemplary one.

Henceforth the stars participate in the daily life of mortals: they are no longer inaccessible: they are mediators between the screen-heaven and earth. Formidable girls, thunderous women, they have established a cult in which admiration supplants veneration. They are less unapproachable, but more moving. Less sublime, but all the more lovable.

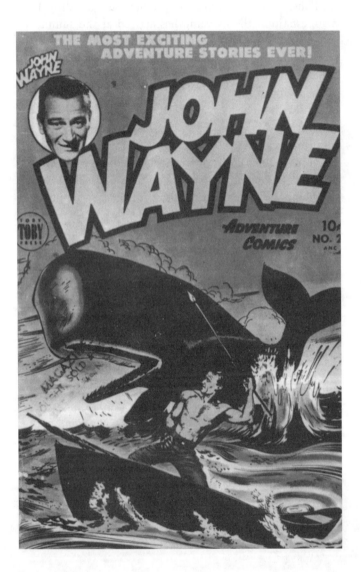

Furthermore, the evolution that degrades the stars' divinity stimulates and multiplies the points of contact between the stars and mortals. Far from destroying their cult, it fosters it. Nearer, more intimate, the star is almost at the disposition of her adorers: hence the profusion of clubs, magazines, photographs, and columns that institutionalize this fervor. A network of channels henceforth drains this collective homage and discharges upon the faithful the thousands of fetishes they crave.

Our stars today are thus the result of an evolution. Of course this evolution has been manifold, complex, and, furthermore, various according to the countries in which it has occurred. We must analyze German stars, Italian stars, French stars, English stars, American stars. We must also confront our "Occidental" evolution with the Oriental, Japanese, Indian, and Egyptian evolutions. In short, we have only suggested the preliminary steps of a general typology of the stars.

But we have seen that, considered as a total phenomenon, the history of the stars repeats, in its own proportions, the history of the gods. Before the gods (before the stars) the mythical universe (the screen) was peopled with specters or phantoms endowed with the glamour and magic of the double.

Several of these presences have progressively assumed body and substance, have taken form, amplified, and flowered into gods and goddesses. And even as certain major gods of the ancient pantheons metamorphose themselves into *hero-gods of salvation*, the star-goddesses humanize themselves and become new mediators between the fantastic world of dreams and man's daily life on earth.

The evolution of the ancient gods corresponds to a profound sociological evolution. Human individuality affirms itself according to an impulse bearing the aspiration to live on the order of the gods, to equal them if possible. The kings were the first to situate themselves on a level with the gods, that is, to consider themselves as *total men*. Subsequently and progressively, the citizens, then the masses, then the slaves have claimed this individuality that men first granted their doubles, their gods, and their kings. *To be recognized as a man is first of all to compel recognition of the right to imitate the gods.*

The new "assimilable" stars, stars as life models, correspond to an increasingly profound desire on the part of the great mass of people for individual salvation; their requirements, at this new stage of individuality, are revealed in a new system of relationships between the real and the imaginary. We can now understand the whole meaning of Margaret Thorp's lucid formula: "This desire to bring the stars down to earth is one of the trends of the times."[3]

Gods and Goddesses

The star is not only an actress. The characters she plays are not only characters. The characters of her films infect the star. Reciprocally, the star herself infects these characters. "People say I'm the same in real life as I am in my movies, and that's why they like me," declares Jean Gabin. This confusion can have far-reaching consequences. A letter was addressed to Charles Boyer in the following way: *Mayerling*, Hollywood, U.S.A. In 1936 the Gary Cooper Fan Club of San Antonio campaigned for their hero's election to the presidency of the United States, arguing that he had clearly demonstrated admirable political aptitude in *Mr. Deeds Goes to Town*.

The news releases of the magazine *Cinémonde* are indicative of this confusion of role and actor: "Hollywood reports that Marlene Dietrich was stabbed between the shoulder blades yesterday, and that Gary Cooper spent the night with the Blue Angel on her ranch." "Micheline Presle abandoned her husband on her wedding night for her next-door neighbor's chauffeur." "Henri Vidal (temporarily) abandons Michèle Morgan for Maria Mauban."

The star determines the many characters of his films; he incarnates himself in them and transcends them. But they transcend him in their turn; their exceptional qualities are reflected back on and illuminate the star. All the heroes Gary Cooper contains within himself direct him to the presidency of the United States, and, reciprocally, Gary Cooper ennobles and enlarges all the heroes he plays: he *garycooperizes* them. Actor and role mutually determine each other. The star is more than an actor incarnating characters, he incarnates *himself in them*, and they become incarnate in him.

The star cannot appear when this reciprocal interpenetration of actor and hero fails to occur. Character actors are not stars: they lend themselves to the most heterogeneous interpretations, but without imposing on them all a unifying personality.

Furthermore, the dialectic of interpenetration that associates certain actors with their roles does not produce a star except in the case of leads and heroes. Carette, Jean Tissier, Dalban, Georgette Anys, Pauline Carton (Parisian tough, sissy, police inspector, matron, old maid) reach only the borders of stardom, interpreting secondary picturesque types and not the heroes of the film.

Yet not every hero is necessarily created by a star. There is a whole segment of film production that cannot afford stars (called B pictures in the United States). Films in this category, especially serials, are rich in marvelous heroes. These heroes are sometimes situated at such an exalted level of myth that they absorb their interpreters without any reciprocity whatever. The interpreters wear out and are replaced without affecting the role (Superman, Tarzan, Zorro). The herculean actor, a Johnny Weissmuller or a Lex Barker, who can manage, even for a moment, to be the equal of his heroic character is extremely rare.

The star appears only at the level of the hero of a major film. The star is absent when powerful economic means are missing, when instead of osmosis there is absorption of the actor by the hero, when there is no lasting connection between actor and role (character parts), or finally when osmosis between character and actor occurs only at the level of a secondary role.

The transferences of actor to character and of character to actor signify neither total identification nor actual duality. If Gary Cooper profits from the innocent sagacity of Mr. Deeds or the virile virtues of the pioneer, he remains Gary Cooper. If Gary Cooper is still Gary Cooper, he assimilates Mr. Deeds and the pioneer into his own personality. Eddie Constantine is and is not Lemmy Caution. Lemmy Caution is and is not Eddie Constantine. The actor does not engulf his role. The role does not engulf the actor. Once the film is over, the actor becomes an actor again, the character remains a character, but *from their union is born a composite creature who participates in both, envelops them both: the star.*

G. Gentilhomme gives an excellent primary definition of the star: "A star appears when the interpreter takes precedence over the character he is playing while profiting by that character's qualities on the mythic level."[1] Which we might complete: "and when the character profits by the star's qualities on this same mythic level." The dialectic of actor and role can account for the star only if the concept of myth is applied. Malraux was the first to explain this phenomenon clearly: "Marlene Dietrich is not an actress, like Sarah Bernhardt; she is a myth, like Phryne."

The word *myth*, itself grown almost mythical in the hands of its many commentators, requires redefinition. A myth is an ensemble of imaginary situations and behaviors. These behaviors and situations may have as their protagonists superhuman beings, heroes, or gods; we can refer to the *myth* of Hercules, or the *myth* of Apollo. But to be exact, Hercules and Apollo are the heroes and the gods *of myths*.

The heroes function halfway between gods and mortals; by the same impulse they aspire to the condition of gods and attempt to deliver mortals from their infinite misery. A kind of mortal avant-garde, the hero is a human being in the process of becoming divine. Related to both gods and men, the heroes of the myths are appropriately called demigods.

The heroes of the movies—heroes of adventure, action, success, tragedy, love, and even, as we shall see, comedy—are, in an obviously attenuated way, mythological heroes in this sense of becoming divine. The star is the actor or actress who absorbs some of the heroic—that is, divinized and mythic—substance of the hero or heroine of the movies, and who in turn enriches this substance by his or her own contribution. When we speak of the *myth* of the star, we mean first of all the process of divinization that the movie actor undergoes, a process that makes him the idol of crowds.

The process is not uniform: there are several types of stars, ranging from the female "romantic" stars (Mary Pickford, Marilyn Monroe) to the comic stars (Fernandel, Chaplin), including the stars of heroism and virile adventure (Douglas Fairbanks, Humphrey Bogart). We shall examine the structures of divinization where they are most striking, at the level of the female star, the romantic heroine; here we can best perceive the originality—the specificity—of the stars' universe.

Love is in itself a divinizing myth: to love passionately is to idealize and to adore. In this sense, all love is a mythic fermentation. The heroes of the movies assume and magnify the myth of love. They purify it of the dross of daily life and bring it to its full flower. The great lovers rule the screen, focusing love's magic on themselves, investing their interpreters with divinizing virtues; they are created to love and be loved, to fasten on themselves that immense affective surge that constitutes the participation of the spectator. The star is above all an actress or an actor who becomes the subject of the myth of love, to the point of instigating a veritable cult.

The actress who becomes a star profits by the divinizing powers of love, but she contributes capital as well: an *adorable* face and body. The star is not only idealized by her role: she is already, at least potentially, ideally beautiful. She is not only magnified by the character she plays, she magnifies it. The two mythic supports, the imaginary heroine and the beauty of the actress, interpenetrate and unite.

Actually, beauty is frequently not a secondary but an essential characteristic of the star. The theater does not require its actors to be beautiful. The star system wants beauties. A certain number of stars are local, national, or international "Miss . . .": Vivianne Romance (Miss Paris), Geneviève Guitry (Miss Cinémonde), Dora Doll, Anne Vernon, Sophie Desmarets, Barbara Laage (finalists in the Miss Cinémonde contest), and so on. The film industry has, furthermore, taken over most of these beauty contests. The title of Miss Universe, awarded under the sponsorship of one of Hollywood's major studios, organized in France by Cinémonde, is worth a starlet's contract to its winner. Any pretty girl can make a movie, so she is told. So she believes (and if there were not so many pretty girls, it would be true). The pinup—that is, the pretty girl who has been photographed—is a potential starlet, and a starlet is a potential star. Beauty is one of the sources of "star quality," and the star system does not content itself with prospecting for it in merely its natural state: it has created or revived the arts of cosmetics, costume, carriage, manners, photography, and, if necessary, surgery, which perfect, prolong, or even produce beauty.

Movie makeup is associated with the movie star to such a degree that the whole modern cosmetic industry is nothing but the offspring of Max Factor and Elizabeth Arden, makeup artists of the Hollywood stars. Heir to the masks and the painted statues of ancient Greece and Oriental civilizations, theater makeup has only incidentally attempted to make faces beautiful. The cinema, on the other hand, uses paints and greases only incidentally in their properly theatrical function. Both the mask, which is an exterior carapace of the face, and the makeup, which molds the face to which it is applied in order to make an adhering mask, function to permit and display a phenomenon of possession. During festivals and sacred rites, the mask reveals a spirit, the incarnation of a genius or a god. Theater makeup perpetuates this function: it differentiates the actor on the stage from profane humanity (which still dresses in a particular way to observe this ceremony) and invests the actor with a sacred and hieratic personality: it indicates that the actor is inhabited by the character he is playing. Makeup's function is also expressive; like the grinning or grimacing mask of the Greek theater, greasepaint fixes the expression, revealing

against a background of tinted skin the movements of the mouth and the eyes enlarged by dark rings.

Let us note that the contemporary theater has diminished the role of makeup; naturalistic plays, the improvement of stage lighting, the size of certain auditoriums, and finally the influence of the cinema itself have combined to efface the hieratic and fatal decor of the face (still preserved in the dance). In the movies, the requirements of the camera image (especially at the period when carbon lights produced ugly violet shadows) demand a certain kind of makeup. But these technical needs are in no way imperative: faces without makeup have illuminated films by Flaherty, Dreyer, Renoir, Rosellini, Visconti. It is above all a question of an aesthetic need that acquired its full significance in relation to the stars. The makeup of the stars is essentially a beauty makeup.

No sooner does the cinema enter what Méliès has called "the theater's spectacular corridor" than it borrows the theater's makeup. But the actor looks less and less "made up" in the movies; actresses, still made up, scarcely look more so than for the usual festivities of life. Of course, greasepaint is still used for special expressive effects: the dark rings around the heroine's eyes when she wakens early after a night of love, the pale lips of the hero on the hospital bed, and so on, but makeup loses its own particular function, which is to make evident the movements of the eyes and the mouth. The close-up will henceforth play this role.

Movie makeup, like street makeup, which is less skillful but which is offered the same skill, restores youth and freshness, repairs the complexion, smooths away wrinkles, compensates for imperfections, and orders the features according to a canon of beauty that can be Hellenic, Oriental, exotic, ingenue, romantic, piquant, feline, and so on.

The star's unalterable beauty implies an unalterable makeup: in darkest Africa as in the filthiest hovel, at grips with hunger, thirst, frostbite, the marvelous Max-Factorized faces bear witness to the presence of the ideal at the heart of the real.

Such makeup obviously depersonalizes the face. Films made without the use of makeup provide the corollary: in the dimensions of the close-up the skin's grain, its shadows and its relief, its thousands of tiny wrinkles transform the countenance into a continent and initiate us into the richest of human geographies. Eisenstein's *Potemkin*, Dreyer's *Joan of Arc*, Poirier's *Verdun* owe a good deal of their expressive power to the absence of makeup. The expression of beauty tends to eliminate expression itself.

But the makeup that diminishes "the eloquence of the face" confers on it a new eloquence. It depersonalizes the star in order to superpersonalize her. Her made-up face is an ideal type. This idealization may be sweetish and emollient, but it is merely the insipidity to which beauty makes all truth subject. Makeup accentuates, stylizes, and definitively achieves a beauty with neither fault nor shadow, perfectly harmonious and perfectly pure.

If need be, a surgeon undertakes to Hellenize the nose: stellar glory sometimes necessitates this nasal assumption. Martine Carol and Juliette Gréco have had to disfigure themselves in this fashion in order to resemble their own ideal faces. Silvana Pampanini has had to have her nose "fixed" three times—the first was a trifle too Bourbon, the second slightly too pug—before it attained those Pythagorean proportions the divine harmonies require. In fact, the archetypal beauty of the star acquires the hieratic quality of the mask; but this mask has become perfectly adherent, identified with the face and dissolved within it.

Movie makeup does not oppose a sacred visage to the profane face of daily life; it raises daily beauty to the level of a superior, radiant, unalterable beauty. The natural beauty of the actress and the artificial beauty of the makeup combine in a unique synthesis. The made-up beauty of the star imposes a unifying personality on her life and her roles.

This is why a star "has no right to be sick or even look out of sorts."[2] She must be permanently identical with herself in all her radiant perfection.

To all the artifices of makeup and plastic surgery are added those of photography. The cameraman must always control the angles of his shots to compensate for the height of the stars who are too short, must always choose the most seductive profile, must always eliminate every infraction of beauty from his field of vision. Projectors redistribute light and shadow over the stars' faces according to the same ideal requirements. Many stars have their preferred cameraman just as they have their personal makeup man, expert at seizing their most perfect image.

The same concern dictates the stars' wardrobe, which must always be perfect in cut, drape, and workmanship. Their costumes stand out against those of the minor actors and the extras, whose clothes symbolize a social status (grocer, professor, garageman, and so on), or else "are conceived

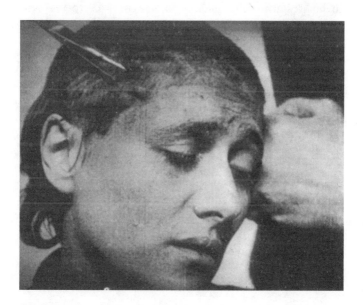

as décors and not individually as are those of the principal characters."[3] Extras wear costumes; the star is dressed. Her clothes are an ornament. In the heart of the Wild West, the star changes her gown for each sequence. Elegance takes precedence over verisimilitude, artifice over realism. Of course the star can be modestly dressed in a raincoat (the cinematic symbol of solitude and feminine destitution) or even wear rags, but raincoat and rags will be made by a master couturier. Lorenian sweaters (*La fille du fleuve*), elegant Lollobrigidian tatters (*Bread, Love and Dreams*) reveal the supreme ornament of the stars: their bodies. The stars are never better dressed than when they are in dishabille.

The requirement of beauty is also a requirement of youth. In the theater, or at the opera, even for the interpretation of adolescent roles, youth matters little: Romeo and Juliet can intertwine their quinquegenarian obesity in lyric duets, and we do not notice the discrepancy. In the American cinema before 1940, the average age of female stars was twenty to twenty-five; their career was shorter than that of male stars, who may ripen, if not age, in order to attain an ideal seductive status.[4]

Subsequently, makeup departments have devoted themselves to rejuvenation with increasing skill: they can suppress wrinkles and restore the complexion to its springtime freshness. Henceforth youth has no age; the continued activity of beauties well over forty is assured (Joan Crawford, Marlene Dietrich, Edwige Feuillère). The stars have accepted time's challenge: still beautiful, they are forever young, forever in love. Has Marlene actually grown old if she can still exhibit her superb body in the casinos of Las Vegas? Yet a day will come when the wrinkles and the puffiness, corrected by ceaseless combat, will be ineffaceable. The star will join her last battle, after which she must resign herself to giving up being in love, that is, being young and beautiful, that is, being a star. Garbo hides her features and, behind the dark glasses, under the turned-up collar, gleams the eternal countenance of "*la divine*."

The mythology of the romantic stars associates moral beauty with physical beauty. The star's ideal body reveals an ideal soul. With the exception of the vamp, whom the star system has eliminated from its solar center, the star cannot be immoral, perverse, bestial.[5] She may deceive us as to her nature at the beginning of the film, but its conclusion must reveal the beauty of her soul.

The star is pure, even—and especially—in love: she lives her passions sincerely and seems "versatile" only because she is in search of the grail of ideal love. She protects children and respects her elders. From the vamp of *Niagara*, Marilyn Monroe has become a star by revealing the maternal heart that her glamorous breast concealed (*River of No Return*).

The star is profoundly good, and this cinematic goodness must be expressed in her private life as well. She cannot be impatient, inattentive, or vague in the eyes of her admirers. She must always help them; she *can* help them because she understands everything. She has the authority,

the heart, and the wit to do so. Her intimate, sentimental, and moral counsels are ceaselessly solicited.

The idealization of the star implies, of course, a corresponding spiritualization. Photographs often show us the star busy painting under the inspiration of the most authentic talent, or else crouching in front of his bookshelves to consult some handsome volume whose splendid binding guarantees the spiritual value. Ray Milland does not conceal the elevation of his preoccupations: "I love astronomy, I love thinking about nature and the possibility of life on other planets. My favorite book is about the vegetation that might exist on the moon. Besides that, I grind away at my 24 volumes of the Encyclopaedia Britannica."

One journalist has come to the conclusion that Robert Montgomery is the modern incarnation of Pico della Mirandola: "There are few philosophical, psychological, political, or sociological works that Bob Montgomery has not studied. He is on friendly terms with Hemingway, Noel Coward, and the most brilliant of today's youth. But he can also hold his own with engineers, doctors, and university professors."

In the dialectic of actor and role, the star contributes her own beauty to the heroine of the film from whom she borrows imaginary moral virtues. Beauty and spirituality combine to form the mythic essence of her personalities, or rather of her superpersonalities. This superpersonality must unceasingly prove itself by appearances: elegance, clothes, possessions, pets, travels, caprices, sublime loves, luxury, wealth, grandeur, refinement—and seasoned to taste with exquisite simplicity and extravagance. Their splendid homes in Beverly Hills, modern Trianons, their elegant apartments in the suburbs of Paris authenticate the superpersonalities of the stars as much as their dazzling, original, and piquant wardrobes.

In the realm of apparel the female star conforms to the supreme etiquette, that of royalty. But like royalty, she too is free to wear a black gown at a reception for Queen Elizabeth.

A royal star, Ava Gardner refuses to curtsy, and smiles at the queen, her equal. Kings and gods maintain order, but may exempt themselves from obeying it. The same applies to the stars. Mistresses of fashion, they transgress its taboos to their heart's desire. Female stars were the first to cross the barriers of the sex of clothes, annexing tweeds, socks, shorts, and slacks; male stars followed suit, adopting unheard-of colors and stripes. The stars know that "*grand chic*" likes to assume the appearances of anti-chic, that the exceptional is sometimes the extremely simple, and that exquisite modesty (a necessary attribute of every great personality) provokes the supreme admiration. The stars *also* love simple dresses, blue jeans, sweaters, leather, and corduroy, which, as much as their more sumptuous dress, set their royal beauty in relief. With touching simplicity the stars eventually cultivate some "artistic" genre that permits their original personalities to express themselves, to the astonishment of the profane. Finally, like the caliphs of Baghdad, who dissimulated their sovereignty under a merchant's cape, the star travels "incognito," supreme ostentation of simplicity. The mere wearing of enormous dark glasses in white frames long permitted the population of Hollywood to recognize the stars. Starlets and extras followed suit, and by dark glasses concealed their anonymity beneath the manifest symbol of celebrity.[6]

Beauty, spirituality, superpersonality, these qualities depend on one another and reciprocally overlap. They constitute the elementary ingredients, doubtless not of all stardom, as we shall see, but of feminine stardom. The star system does not merely reveal such qualities: it perfects them, refreshes them, even fabricates them altogether. Beauty alone is required at the outset, and even nonugliness provides a raw material for the creation of beauty. Spirituality and personality, of course, can be manufactured out of whole cloth. Furthermore, it is the admiring crowds, in this last instance, who confer such qualities on the star and who by this attribution of a soul will *make* her a star.

At the outset, anyone endowed with that gratuitous and irreplaceable talent that is beauty can aspire to become a star. Every pretty girl can say, "Why not me?" Technique is essential to a career on the stage, but no previous training is required to be a star. In offices, in high schools, over the counters of department stores, at the heart of all worry and all waiting, at the summit of every dream of glory, the captive beauty feeds and fosters one ultimate dream: "I will be a star." Sometimes she breaks her chains and signs up for one glamour course or another: the waiting room of the promised annunciation.

Why not me? The examples are innumerable: a young girl encountered in the street or on the subway, accosted ("Would you like to make a movie, miss?"), an extra, a model, a pinup, a winner or even a loser of a beauty contest becomes Sylvana Mangano, Ava Gardner, Gina Lollobrigida. Everything promises . . . But at the same time everything discourages: in twelve years only twelve extras out of twenty thousand have become stars in Hollywood. Among the millions who are called, few are chosen.

To be a star is precisely the impossible made possible, the possible made impossible. The most talented actress can never be assured of becoming a star, but an unknown pretty face may be given a leading role from one day to the next. (The most talented actress, however, *can* become a star, and the pretty face has every chance of remaining unknown until it fades.)

The myth begins here, outside the kingdom of the stars, at the very heart of reality. The star system is closed, inaccessible. At the gates of the castle, Uncles Talky and St. John-Goldmouth discourage every hope and prophesy disillusion, unemployment, poverty. And yet they also encourage the Cinderellas and ugly ducklings by pointing out how the other Cinderellas and ugly ducklings were discovered and summoned by the messengers from the castle. A remarkable technique of encouragement-discouragement:

accession to stardom depends on luck; luck is a break, and a break is grace.

Hence, no recipe. The handbooks with promising titles (*Tu serás star, Comment devenir vedette de cinéma*, and so on) stress this point. What matters is the *gift*—that is, the gift of oneself as much as that miraculous and transcendent gift, the gift of grace.

Beauty and youth are the first conditions of grace. With these qualities given, the handbooks urge the candidates to develop beauty, to exploit their youth as soon as possible. They do not recommend any preparation for an actor's career, but provide, wrapped in modest precautions, several arriviste techniques. One gentleman declares that self-assurance is useful ("they will end up hiring you to get rid of a monumental pest"); he warns against "sleeping around," but bears witness to the fact that "great stars exercise a rather advanced form of intimacy with certain persons in prominent positions." All means are good in so noble a cause. Becoming a star justifies itself like reasons of state, like any supreme success that transforms hustling into ambition, ambition into greatness of soul.

Glamour courses and beauty contests are traps in which grace may be ensnared. Beauty contests can lead directly to the studio gates and immediate "starletization": after much sifting, the title of Miss Universe is accorded simultaneously with a Hollywood contract.

Glamour courses are nurseries of another kind. "Learn how to act," says the director of one of them to his students; but candidates for stardom know that they are merely marking time in one of those privileged places where grace likes to make its elections. They know that before everything else they must make known their beauty, their "personality," their "type." Here face, bust, hips, legs are the most eloquent signs of "personality," signs that lead them toward the action of grace.

Movie directors sometimes visit these establishments, sometimes run an announcement in newspapers, occasionally even walk through towns and villages looking for a new face. Hollywood has invented the talent scout, a specialized detector of future stars, who combs the countryside in mysterious anonymity, searching for the sources of star-making radioactivity.

A talent scout is struck by a promising face in the subway. Proposition, test photo, test recording. If the tests are conclusive, the young beauty leaves for Hollywood. Immediately put under contract, she is refashioned by the masseurs, the beauticians, the dentists, even the surgeons. She learns to walk, loses her accent, is taught to sing, to dance, to stand, to sit still, to "hold herself." She is instructed in literature, ideas. The foreign star whom Hollywood cuts back to starlet level sees her beauty transformed, recomposed, Max-Factorized, and she learns American. Then there are more tests: among others, a thirty-second close-up in Technicolor. There is new winnowing out. She is noticed, approved, and given a minor role. Her car, her servants, her dogs, her goldfish, her birds are chosen for her. Her personality grows more complex, becomes enriched. She waits for letters. Nothing. Failure. But one day or the next the Fan Mail Department might notify the executive producer that she is receiving three hundred letters a day from admirers. The studio decides to launch her and fabricates a fairy tale of which she is the heroine. She provides material for the columnists; her private life is already illuminated by the glare of the projectors. At last she is given the lead in a major film. Apotheosis: the day when her fans tear her clothes—she is a star.

This is how an admirable industrial Pygmalionism produces such splendid goddesses as Ava Gardner. The star is manufactured:

"Get me a star."
"Usual budget?"
"Usual budget."[7]

Fed by the talent scouts, a veritable star production line snaps up the unknown girl in the street in order, after numerous manipulations, mountings, cuttings, splicings, eliminations, selections, to project a star on the screens of the world.

We can see during the course of this process the flowering of the divinity that was germinating within the limits of mere beauty. Three planetary orbits mark off the interstellar distance that leads from the pretty girl to the star. These are not necessary stages, and each can be a terminus: pinup, starlet, and star, The pinup is a pretty girl who makes a profession of being photographed. Her beauty is already profitable, effective. The pinup, like the star, is already public.

But the pinup is unknown. She must remain anonymous. Her name is never indicated under the photograph. She is a plastic material for new attitudes, forever new metamorphoses among which it is scarcely possible to identify her. The pinup has no identity in either sense of the term: she must never resemble herself, she has no "herself." The star, on the other hand, is always recognized and recognizable. Her archetypal personality always transcends her attitudes and her roles.

The photographs that reproduce the body of the pinup and those that reproduce the body of the star are of a different nature. At least they were until the appearance of the Marilynian type, that remarkable synthesis of star and pinup, which we will not neglect to examine in every detail. The pinup emphasizes her body, her breasts, her hips, her flesh. The star exhibits her nudity only at rare and decisive moments. Margaret Thorp points out that *a star's importance is in inverse proportion to the amount of leg shown in her photographs*. Of course, she climbs the ladder to stardom by pinup poses, sunbaths, and swimming pools. She has reached the top when she is photographed in hostess gowns. It is then that the star exhibits her soul and her face, in which eroticism unites with spirituality.

The pinup is all legs and bust. Faces too are displayed on

magazine covers, but in front of these faces without identities, each man dreams of the face he loves, like the prisoners in *Brute Force*. The pinup is indeterminate. The star is superdetermined. The manufacture of stars essentially consists of inflating the original pinup with personality.

The starlet is halfway between the pinup and the star. The starlet was originally almost-a-star, but in general today any young girl is called a starlet, even if she has never made a picture, provided she has an immense desire to be a star and gets herself photographed with a mention of her name. A starlet is thus a pretty girl who manages to get herself known as such—who imposes her name.

The starlet is in search of the attributes of personality. Summoned into being by the myth of the star, she does everything in her power to fulfill its conditions. Like the star, she must change her wardrobe as often as possible, attend cocktail parties, receptions, and so on. She goes to the Cannes Festival, where she prefers a small room at the Carlton to an opulent suite at a middle-class hotel. In Cannes, the starlet attempts to display an unrivaled individuality: we find her walking a lamb on the beach or leading a leopard to dinner on a leash (1955). Unfortunately, she is compelled to adopt pinup poses for the photographer. She would like to imitate the star's comportment, but she is obliged to do the reverse: whereas the star flees her admirers, the starlet must look for hers, even create them; whereas the star reveals her soul, the starlet must exhibit her body, offering it as a sacrifice on the altar guarded by the film merchants. The battle for exhibition possibilities among starlets results in the strangest, least natural, but always most stereoscopic poses. Starlet Simone Silva bares her breasts and submits them to palpable appreciation; the star Gina Lollobrigida permits hers to be merely guessed at. The starlet takes her chances of becoming a star by means of the very photographs and attitudes that the star refuses.

But she is talked about, and thereby climbs the first

rungs to stardom. She makes her personality known. This personality is still a fragile one. When the star appears, the starlet dissolves into the landscape; she loses her individuality, becomes a pinup again, surviving in a cohesive collection of pretty girls, the star's maids of honor, lady cardinals of a papacy to which each in turn hopes to be summoned.

On a higher level comes the lead, although the lead is still not the intermediary echelon between the starlet and the star. The lead is the common status of all actors of the first rank. Stars are leads, of course, but leads such as Charles Vanel, Escande, or Larquey can become stars only as an exception. What they lack is that extra quality that transforms personality into superpersonality. The star, like the queen bee, differentiates herself by acquiring a royal jelly of superpersonality. We shall see farther on that there are many roads that lead to this superpersonality. What concerns us here is the case—at once extreme, particular, and significant—of the female romantic star, for whom the star system is an enormous, impersonal personality-mill, starting with the raw materials of beauty and youth.

The interchange and identification of the two personalities, that of the heroine of the film and the more or less fabricated one of the actress, produce the star, who in return will determine the characters she is to incarnate.

Henceforth we embark upon the stellar dialectic. The star's beauty and youth magnify her roles as lover and heroine. Her love and heroism magnify in turn the young and beautiful star. In the movies she incarnates a private life. In private she must incarnate a movie life: by means of each of her film characterizations the star interprets herself; by revealing her own character, she interprets the heroines of her films.

What is a film if not a "romance," that is, a personal story destined for the public? The star's personal life must be public. Magazines, interviews, parties, confessions (*Film de ma vie*) force the star to display her person, her gestures, her tastes. The stars have no secrets: one explains how she avoids constipation, another reveals the secret joy she experiences from pulling ticks out of her griffon's ears. Gossip columns, indiscretions, photographs transform the magazine reader into a voyeur, as if at a movie itself. The reader-voyeur persecutes the star in every sense of the term. Ingrid Bergman and Rita Hayworth may evade photographers, but are somehow always caught. Telecameras are hidden behind privet hedges in the park and capture the moment when Grace Kelly kisses Jean-Pierre Aumont's hand.

There is no hiding place for the star. If she dares protest, bitter echoes creep into the magazine articles, her fans grow indignant. She is a captive of her fame. In Hollywood, the star system demands the systematic organization of the private-public life of the stars. Buster Keaton was condemned by the terms of his contract never to laugh in public. Contracts similarly constrain the ingenue to a life of chastity, at least in appearance, and the constant companionship of her mother. The glamour girl, on the other hand, must repeatedly be seen in nightclubs on the arm of one cavalier after another chosen by her producers. Impresarios arrange the stars' intimate and romantic rendezvous, illuminated by moonlight and flashbulbs.

The star belongs altogether to her public—a glorious servitude that arouses the pity of the very public that demands it. Like kings, like gods, the star belongs even more to her admirers than they belong to her. Her adorers demand of her both simplicity and magnificence. The one is inadequate without the other, as we have seen: the height of grandeur is exquisite simplicity, but such simplicity would be invisible if it were really simple. It must therefore be ostentatious.

We have already suggested the luxury with which the stars surround themselves "in all simplicity." Luxury, of course, means expense. Men labor; kings and gods spend. And what they spend is this very labor of men who do not spend but labor for this vicarious expense, which they will enjoy in dreams, as spectators.

Expense means play. The stars of the great epoch who spent without counting the cost played away their lives. Today's stars invest their revenues more prosaically. But they still live a life of play. Work was banished from the Elysian Fields, which the heroes attained after rigorous trials. Similarly, after the labors of a cinematic Hercules, the private life of the star is a life of holidays and receptions, a round of parties.

Hollywood's social life, a life of pleasures, revolves around these parties.[8] This life, mythical for the laboring moviegoer, is quite real in Hollywood; rendezvous, idylls, frolics, masquerades, "come as you are" parties, "come as your first ambition" parties, and so on. A life without limits. To take a plane across continents to make location shots, to turn up at a premiere or a "festival" is the exaltation of a superior freedom. Making a film ultimately appears to be the game of games.

This life of play, this carnival life—disguised, licentious, lavishing photographs, gossip, and rumors like flowers and confetti—attains its fullness and mythic peak at the festivals. The star system has devoured the international film contests and turned them into international star contests. At Cannes, it is no longer the films but the stars that are exhibited as the chief attraction. It is obvious that the Festival is above all, in the opinion of a public that the daily press and the movie magazines form or inform, a rendezvous of the stars, as well as of everyone who participates in the star system (directors, famous writers, wealthy playboys, Aly Khans) and also of everyone who aspires to stardom (starlets, pinups, budding geniuses).

During the Anthesteries the dead return among the living; similarly, during the yearly Cannes Festival, the impalpable stars leave the screen and offer themselves to mortal eyes. They condescend to have a body, a smile, an earthly gait, and even distribute tangible proof of their incarnation: autographs.

The first question put to anyone returning from the Cannes Festival is "What stars did you see?" and only afterward, "What films?" The initiate modestly instances: "Lollobrigida, Loren, Constantine," and then he must answer the second question, the key question, the question that implies and explains the whole mythology of the Festival: "Is she as pretty in real life as she is on the screen—as exciting, as provocative?" and so on. For the real problem is the confrontation of myth and reality, appearance and essence.

The Festival, by its ceremony and its glamorous mise-en-scène, attempts to prove to the universe that the stars are faithful to their image. Everything in the Festival's internal economy as well as in its daily manifestations indicates that for the stars there is not, on one hand, a private, everyday, and banal life and, on the other, an ideal and glorious image. It proves that the actual, physical life of the stars is consistent to love. The star is wholly submerged in her image and is compelled to lead a cinematic life. Cannes is the mystic site of this identification of the imaginary and the real.

The stars lead a festival existence: the Festival leads a life of stars—a movie life. Ceremonies, receptions, battles of flowers, bathing suits, evening dresses reveal them: décolleté, half naked under a perpetual sun that tries to make itself worthy of the klieg lights (the climate of Cannes, like that of Venice, lends its geographic charm to the localization of the myth of the star). These marvelous images are of an exquisite spontaneity, although of course quite as prepared, as ritual, as those of the films. Everything contributes to the image they present of life as Elysium. "Impose" is perhaps the mot juste here, for it is not so much a matter of appearing to the Cannes public as a matter of appearing to the whole universe through the intermediaries of photographs, television, and newsreels.

From the apprentice starlet to the sovereign star, from the bucolic dishabille of the Lerin Islands to the formal dinner at Les Ambassadeurs, everything begins and ends with the photograph. Everything that is photogenic aspires to be photographed. Everything that has been photographed resembles everything that has been filmed. Everything that has been filmed is multiplied by photography. More than one hundred photographers crowd around the square, each carrying on his shoulder the eyes of millions of voyeurs. It is the *double* of the Festival universe that matters: seized by

the magnesium flashes, it will be distributed like a mystical pabulum throughout the world. It is the appearance, the beauty, the fake eternity, the myth of the star-who-lives-the-film-of-her-life, the magic cinema, that rule at Cannes for fifteen days. We must therefore interrogate the thousands of photographs, or rather the several photographic archetypes with their thousands of variants, that the Festival diffuses throughout the world.

The Festival staircase, swept, watered, and gleaming under the projectors, is dominated by a veritable reef of cameramen. At its foot, in an enclosure formed by barricades and police, the stars are deposited by their tremendous limousines. Then begins the mystical, radiant, smiling ascension. This ceremony, an equivalent of the Roman triumph and the ascension of the virgin, is repeated daily. It is the great rite. The star is *there*, at her moment of extreme magic efficacy, between the limousine and the movie theater where she will double herself, between the screen and the temple. The key photograph at the Festival is the one that seizes her in this radiance and this glory at the apogee of the ceremonies.

The other photographs are devoted to receptions, beach parties, the Carlton bar, and other consecrated sites. Yet they do not neglect unexpected profane regions that the star might sanctify with her presence. These photographs enshrine a veritable ritual of poses and attitudes. The typical poses express the plenitude and ecstatic joy of life: a proferred and radiant face, a laugh opening not upon the obscene orifice of the palate but on a superb row of clenched teeth. This synthesis of laugh and smile communicates the euphoria of the former without its vulgarity, the friendliness of the latter without its reserve. Stars, starlets, and pinups alike smile at life and, more personally, at us.

Another classic attitude: the amiable, intertwined, and tender poses that bear witness to marvelous friendships and even more marvelous loves. The star's life is steeped in love.

Not content with capturing prepared romances, the tele-camera attempts to surprise the real kisses and caresses exchanged by the stars when they think they are in private.

A third series of photographs situates itself in the moving tradition of the Virgin with Child. The star (Lollo-brigida, Doris Day) is shown kissing a little girl, preferably a star herself (Brigitte Fossey). These images prove that the star, profoundly human, is always ready to pour out the milk of her maternal tenderness upon all that is innocent, weak, disarmed. At the same time, these photographs reflect the evolution of the star system: within the last twenty-five years the star has lost certain divine attributes (proud, inaccessible solitude, an unmatched destiny working itself out entirely within the compass of the sacred sentiments of love and death) in order to acquire more familiar attributes (domestic preoccupations, a taste for fried potatoes, love of children). Less like statues but more touching, the human stars are less idolized but more beloved.

Finally, we must note the increased importance of comic or piquant poses and attitudes: Gina Lollobrigida bowling, Eddie Constantine in a chef's hat tasting sauces, and the like. These charming gestures gloss the myth of the stars' happiness, a vacation happiness of laughter and games that the Elysian Fields reserved for heroes.

Carefree pleasures and games, the enjoyment of the bizarre, love, and ecstatic joy in life itself are thus the characteristics of a world qualitatively overpriced and overvalued, swept clean of all imperfections, ugliness, drudgery, or despair, a life under the sign of a permanent festival.

The official rendezvous of the stars in a landscape of budding starlets derives both from the theater and from ritual. Or rather from the great spectacle of superproduction. Gary Cooper and Gisèle Pascal, Olivia de Havilland and Pierre Galante, Grace Kelly and Jean-Pierre Aumont enact, as in the movies, on a movie set, and beyond the movies, the mystery of fatal love.

The star adheres most effectively to her screen character in affairs of the heart. The romance of Greta Garbo and John Gilbert, of Michèle Morgan and Henri Vidal, born from movie kisses, shines at the mythic zenith of the star system.

It is preferable that a star love a star: Fairbanks-Pickford, Gable-Lombard, Taylor-Stanwyck, Pellegrin-Pascal, Marchal-Robin, Sinatra-Gardner, Granger-Simmons, Signoret-Montand, and so on, make model couples. Only kings, aristocrats, heavy-weight champions, bullfighters, band leaders, nabobs, Aly Khans, Rainiers, Stokowskis, and Dominguins are situated at the stars' level.

The star suffers, divorces, is happy, even *lives* for love. Her adorers are not jealous of her lovers, or rather only of those who take her away from the movies. Then the deceived and betrayed fans curse Rita Hayworth and Ingrid Bergman, who have abandoned them.

The star can pass from affair to affair on condition that she remain faithful to love's great collective rendezvous in the movie palaces. Her marriage rouses the liveliest sympathy, her divorce an even greater one. "An actress's mail generally increases after a divorce, according to numerous fan mail departments in Hollywood."[9] Actually, the fans expect the star's divorce as soon as she marries.

As on the screen, so in life: love cannot take a holiday. In Hollywood, "four hundred reporters, without counting the native gossip mongers, are on the alert 24 hours a day, ceaselessly on the trail of flirtations, liaisons, divorces, infidelities."[10]

Hollywood introduces into its stars' real adventures whatever amount of fiction it can get away with, entirely fabricating certain rumors of felicity or impending divorce according to its box-office requirements, ceaselessly elaborating fictitious love affairs with appropriate partners. The studios themselves often pick up the checks for these "romantic" dinners and cocktails. "X is going out a lot with

Y," it is written, and everything is understood, hoped for or feared. During the 1937–38 season, Tyrone Power was actually credited with the tenderest feelings, in succession, for Loretta Young, Sonja Henie, Janet Gaynor, Simone Simon, and Arleen Whelan.

Love thus manufactured is evidently created in the image of love in the movies themselves: a passionate sentiment impregnated with spirituality. Of course the myth of the stars does not deny sexuality. Sexuality is always understood. The gossip columns imply it in their myriad "engagements" or "violent attractions." But the stars make love only as a result of a superior and desperate impulse of the soul. Priestesses of love, they transcend it in accomplishing it. They cannot give themselves up to debauch—that is, to pleasure without spirituality—except under penalty of banishment from Beverly Hills. They must at least pretend. But even then they do not escape the nyctalopic eye of *Confidential*, which offers their secret lives as a feeding ground to the wood lice of voyeurism.

The star enjoys life and love on behalf of the whole world. She has the mystical greatness of the sacred prostitute. In the Lethe of each dark auditorium her body purifies and immolates itself. Her partners are of little consequence: it is Love who visits her, Love she is waiting for, Love who guides her.

The festival quality of the stars' private-public life, the great love affairs, are obviously collective myths simultaneously secreted by the public and fabricated by the star system. But this mythical life, we repeat, is in part actually lived by the star herself.

The star is in effect subjectively determined by her double on the screen. She is nothing since her image is everything. She is everything since she is this image too. The psychology of the stars requires a brief incursion into the psychology of the dual personality.

There is a primary moment of human evolution in which the double corresponds to a fundamental life experience: among primitive man as among children, the first self-consciousness is exterior to the self. The "I" is first of all an other, a *double*, revealed and localized in shadows, reflections, mirrors. The double awakens when the body sleeps, is liberated and becomes a "spirit" or phantom when the body will never awaken again. It survives the mortal body. The gods will free themselves from the common lot of the dead in order to become the great immortals. At the origin of the god is the double.

At our present stage of civilization, our double has atrophied. Our language reveals certain residual traces: the formula "Me" is one of these residues. The double has pasted himself against us, has become our "character," the pretentious role we unceasingly play, as much for ourselves as for anyone else. The duality is ultimately internalized: it is a dialogue with our soul, our conscience. The star, on the contrary, sees this archaic double resuscitate, detach itself from her, and unfurl on the screen: it is her own image, omnipresent, spellbinding, dazzling. Like her admirers, the star is subjugated by this image superimposed on her real self: like them, too, she wonders if she is really identical with her double on the screen. Devalued by her double, a phantom of her phantom, the star can escape her own emptiness only by amusing herself and can amuse herself only by imitating her double, by miming her movie life. An inner necessity impels her to assume her role completely, to live a life of love and festivals. She must keep abreast of her double. Thus the screen mythology extends itself behind the screen and beyond it. The star is drawn into a dialectic of division and reunification of the personality, as is the actor, the writer, and the politician. Every actor tends to accentuate this doubling (even taking a pseudonym) and at the same time tries to surmount it; he frequently ends by playing his role in life and becoming a ham. The star is not a ham: she does not play a role exterior to herself; like a queen, she lives her own role.

Like the writer, the star admires herself, adores herself. But middle age, or at least maturity, is the time of the writer's full glory, the stage actor's widest fame. That of the star is fragile, always threatened, always ephemeral. Like Abu Hassan in *The Thousand and One Nights*, the queen-for-perhaps-a-day fears waking.

Hence the stars bluff, exaggerate, spontaneously divinize themselves, not only "for publicity's sake," as is prosaically said, not only to equal their double, but also to support its ephemeral survival, to reanimate their faith in themselves. It is always from a melange of faith and doubt that the passions derive. Because everything compels her simultaneous belief and doubt, the star must nourish her own myth.[11] She lives in the marvelous. The films with which the producers and writers are discontented are for her the "world's greatest," "better than ever," and, of course, "marvelous."[12]

Hollywood is indeed the city of the marvelous, in which the mythic life is real and real life mythic. Here are the Elysian Fields: a legendary city, but also a city *living* its legend. A ship of dreams anchored in real life. A California Shangri-La from which flows the elixir of immortality.

The Stellar Liturgy

Worshipped as heroes, divinized, the stars are more than objects of admiration. They are also subjects of a cult. A religion in embryo has formed around them. This religion diffuses its frenzies over most of the globe. No one who frequents the dark auditoriums is really an atheist. But among the moviegoing masses can be distinguished the sect of the faithful who wear relics and otherwise consecrate themselves to worship, the fanatics, the fans.

We must consider separately the fanatics to whom nothing that happens in front of the camera is alien and the star worshippers. This second category constitutes the idolatrous mass of the fans, which can be estimated at 5 or 6 percent of the total population in France, England, and the United States. Their cult primarily subsists on specialized publications. Although there are no theater magazines, dance magazines, or even music magazines devoted entirely to actors, dancers, or singers, movie magazines are devoted essentially to the stars. In regular, official, and intimate communication with the kingdom of the stars, these publications pour out on the faithful all the vivifying elements of their faith: photographs, interviews, gossip, romanticized biographies, and so on.

One channel is still more direct, more personal, more stirring than the movie magazine, although it may make use of the latter's columns: the stars' mail. Stage actors, dancers, and singers all receive a considerable number of letters from their admirers, but the star's mail far exceeds this correspondence in quantity and is distinguished by its contents as well. Letters addressed to Hollywood stars can be estimated at several million a year. One major studio received in 1939 from fifteen thousand to forty-five thousand letters or cards a month, minimum figure in comparison with other years. According to Margaret Thorp, a major star receives three thousand letters a week.

In France, relations between stars and their admirers are direct. In the United States, the studios manage the fan mail departments, veritable meteorological services that regard the number of letters a star receives as an exact barometer of her popularity. This barometer will permit us to take account of some of the high mystical pressures that sustain the star system.

Fan clubs are the chapels in which particular passions are raised to a frenzy. The idol periodically comes to sanctify her club, revealing to it new aspects of her private-public life, of her cinematic activities. She answers the questions that are fired at her, she sings, dances, organizes some collective excursion. Jean Marais takes his admirers for a ride in the *bateau-mouche*. The clubs' resources, like those of churches, are expended in part on charitable works, in part on the propagation of the faith. The bronze effigy of Luis Mariano is distributed among the faithful. Each star has her special cult. There are clubs democratically open to any admirer who wishes to join, others of a more esoteric character. Membership in the Deanna Durbin club was limited to an elite. To belong, a member

had to have seen each of Deanna Durbin's films at least twice;

had to present an important collection of documents
  about the star;
had to subscribe to the *Deanna Journal*.

The Joan Crawford Club was one of the best organized;
each candidate received the following letter:

Dear Inquirer:

Thank you so much for your request for information
about our organization. I shall be glad to tell you all about
it, and I do hope that you will be interested.

The official Joan Crawford Club was organized in
September 1931 and is today one of the oldest and largest
active clubs in existence. We have members in all sections
of this country, as well as in many distant parts of the
world, England, Ireland, Australia, Scotland, South Africa,
and even Java included.

Miss Crawford takes a keen interest in all of our
activities. Not only does she send personally autographed
pictures to all of our new members, but she writes a long
letter to the members for each edition of our club
publication; and she also answers your questions about her
in "Joan's Question Box," a regular feature of the magazine.

We are really quite proud of our magazine, which
includes many interesting articles about Miss Crawford
and our honorary members; club news, gossip, and the
latest news, of Hollywood, New York, and London, the
entertainment centers of the world. We do have a regular
editorial staff comprised of the members of the club, and
we cordially invite anyone who wishes to do so to submit
articles to our magazine. Among our contributors to each
edition are Jerry Asher and Katherine Albert, two of Miss
Crawford's best friends, both professional writers who are
able to tell us many interesting things about her.

Membership entitles you to a personally autographed
picture of Miss Crawford, a membership card,

membership list, six issues of "The Crawford News" which is published every other month, and all other club privileges. The dues are fifty cents a year for domestic members and seventy-five cents, or three shillings, for foreign members, payable by an International Money Order.

I hope that I shall soon have the pleasure of welcoming you as a fellow member of our club.

Sincerely yours,
Marian L. Dommer
Acting President[1]

At the feet of each star rises, as if of its own accord, a chapel—that is, a club. Some swell into cathedrals like the Luis Mariano club, which includes more than twenty thousand zealots. In the United States, each church periodically organizes pilgrimages to the great mother-Jerusalem, Hollywood.

Festivals are the great Corpus Christi Days when the star descends in person to witness her triumph. On such occasions fervor can mount to frenzy, adoration to delirium.

Magazines, photographs, correspondence, clubs, pilgrimages, ceremonies, festivals are the fundamental institutions of the cult of the stars. We must now examine this cult itself.

The fans' love cannot *possess*, in either the sociological or the physical sense of the word. The star escapes private appropriation. Love for the stars is a love without jealousy, without envy, divisible among them, relatively unsexualized—that is, a matter of adoration. Adoration implies an earthworm-star relation, but it is generally established within a real love between two human beings, and in complete reciprocity. The adorer wants the adored to be an adorer herself; the earthworm wants to be a star in his turn. The fan, however, accepts himself purely and simply as an earthworm. He wants to be loved, but quite humbly. It is this inequality that characterizes religious love, adoration that is not reciprocal but eventually recompensed.

The letters sent to the stars express this adoration, the magazines and photographs nourish it, the clubs institutionalize it. The letters make constant use of the same phrases: "You are my favorite star. . . . I've seen your last film six, seven, eight times." One correspondent vouches for the fact that he has seen the same film 130 times. The letters are lauds, raptures, ecstasy, professions of faith.

An investigation conducted by J. P. Mayer among British moviegoers chosen at random and not among the declared fanatics of the stars provides a series of testimonials in which the language of love ("I am in love with . . .") is mingled with that of adoration ("my idol"). It may be useful to quote from some of them:[2]

age: 22   sex: female   nationality: British
occupation: office worker
At seventeen I was very interested in great love stories.
Tyrone Power was my idol and I saw his pictures three and
four times. I think I must have fallen in love with him as I
spoke quite a lot about him to my sister and friends until
they got sick of me talking about him. I like his manner in
acting, lovemaking, his courage and daring. When he kisses
his leading lady a funny thrill runs up my spine to the heart.
Sometimes in dreams which seem very real, I imagine he
is kissing me. This may sound ridiculous but it is quite
true and is the way I feel. Tyrone Power to me is a very
good swordsman which seems to suit his personality. I
have seen every one of his pictures to his last (*Crash Dive*)
before he joined the Marines. I miss seeing him on the
screen very much and hope to see him again in very near
future. I envy his lovely wife Annabella, but I like her
because she is very charming and is a very good actress.

age: 22   sex: female   nationality: British
occupation: secretary
It was in my early teens that I first fell in love—and that

was with Jan Kiepura, whom I had seen in *Tell Me Tonight*.
Love? Infatuation you would say! And I suppose you are
right. But it was heartbreakingly real to me. I was assured
by adults that I would soon grow out of that phase. But
no! All through my teens I continued falling in love with
one film star after another. And each time was sheer
torture—a desperate longing to be made love to by them
all. Sometimes it would last for days, sometimes for weeks
or even months, awakened and anew each time I saw
them. Nobody knew just how miserable I felt. . . . And yet,
looking back, it was all so real to me that I don't think I
would otherwise have known such complete and utter
happiness as when I used to dream that one day I could
meet those people. I believe it must have been the effect
of those desperate infatuations that has altered my outlook
on love. . . . I soon found that the attentions of the local
boy irritated me. I was contemptuous of his rather dull
dates, and felt that his ordinary advances were childish and
inexperienced. . . . And yet I have finished some really
very pleasant friendships because of this intangible
longing for something different: something based, I
suppose, on my very early idea of love.

age: 22   sex: female   nationality: British
profession: medical student
[Deanna Durbin] became my first and only screen *idol*. I
collected pictures of her and spent hours sticking them in
scrapbooks. I would pay any price within the range of my
pocket money for a book, if it had a new picture, however
tiny, of her in it. I adored her and my adoration influenced
my life a great deal. I wanted to be as much like her as
possible, both in my manners and clothes. Whenever I
was to get a new dress, I would find from my collection a
particularly nice picture of Deanna and ask for a dress like
she was wearing. I did my hair as much like hers as I could
manage. If I found myself in any annoying or aggravating

situation . . . I found myself wondering what Deanna
would do and modified my own reactions accordingly. She
had far more influence on me than any amount of lectures
and rows from parents. I went to all her films. . . . Once, I
remember a re-issue of *Three Smart Girls* was showing at
another town about twelve miles across country from ours
. . . I was finally allowed to go and thoroughly enjoyed
myself watching "my Deanna" as I called her: I bought all
the records she made and played them over and over again.

age: 20   sex: female   nationality: British
occupation: milliner
I have fallen in love with my screen idol. He is a
newcomer to films, his name is Gene Kelly. I first fell in
love with him when I seen him in *For Me and My Gal*
which I seen four times and could see it again and again.
I saw *Cover Girl* five times. I have a picture of Gene Kelly
sent direct from MGM, Hollywood. . . . I really fell for
Gene when he had that love scene with Judy Garland in
For Me and My Gal. The scene where they had that long
kiss which made Judy Garland clench her fists (until her
knuckles shown white, I suppose). I'll never forget that.

age: 30   sex: female   nationality: British
occupation: mother of three children
At sixteen I was in love with Ramon Navarro, Ronald
Colman, and others. But Nelson Eddy is now the only star
that still makes my heart beat, because of his magnificent,
magical voice.

age: 37   sex: female   nationality: British
occupation: factory worker
Then I was in the flapper age when Rudolph Valentino
was the hero. . . . I know we girls had to stand to get in
(*The Sheik*) and we were saying "Isn't he marvelous?" "I
wish I was Agnes Ayers." I bought every photo I could

possibly get of him, and my bedroom was surrounded with him. . . . Even now when I see old pictures of him . . . I still get a little romantic feeling.

age: 19   sex: female   nationality: British
occupation: factory worker
At about fifteen I fell in love with Conrad Veidt. At the time he represented my idea of a perfect man—handsome,

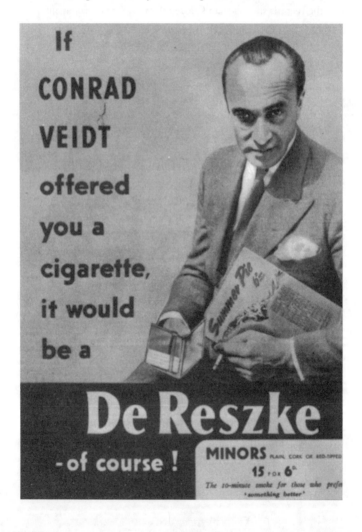

distinguished, cultured, intelligent, an attractive foreign accent, a perfect lover. . . . Moreover, he was nearly always the villain who I think is infinitely more attractive than the insipid hero. This infatuation died with him.

age: 17   sex: female
When the war started I was eleven and my idol was Tyrone Power. Now my other favorite is James Mason who I think is very seductive. I love his voice and his looks and I think he is very handsome. I don't know why I love him but I know no one can take his place except Van Johnson.

age: 26   sex: female   nationality: British
I only fell in love once with a movie actor. It was Conrad Veidt. His magnetism and his personality got me. His voice and gestures fascinated me. I hated him, feared him, loved him. When he died it seemed to me that a vital part of my imagination died too, and my world of dreams was bare.

age: 19   sex: female   nationality: British
occupation: factory worker
Did I ever fall in love with my screen idol—I'll say! Most impressionable kids do. At fourteen I thought Mickey Rooney perfect, at fifteen I was crazy about Robert Taylor, and at sixteen Clark Gable was tops. I still like him, and friends often wonder how I can like Gable and Sinatra so much when they are so totally different. But I do.

age: 23   sex: female   occupation: laboratory assistant
Each of us (at school) had a favorite, with Bing Crosby in the lead. Bing's photographs were very scarce, because of the great demand. I had no particular favorite, until one night, I saw *Queen Christina*. From then on I was a Garbo fan. I followed her career with great interest and made a point of seeing her films, until *Two-Faced Woman*, and after that, I bothered no more about her.

age: 18   sex: female   nationality: British

My favorite at the moment is Bing Crosby. . . . I think of him constantly: I wonder what his reactions are to certain news items; I try to imagine what he is doing at different times during the day; I plan various films for him, and think up ideas for his radio show. I wonder how his wife and kids are, and I wish I could meet him some day before he gets any older.

I listen to people's conversations about him, read every news item about him, study the daily newspaper to see what time he is broadcasting, and plan my day as far as possible not to interfere with my listening. When two programs, which might possibly feature Bing, are broadcast simultaneously on different wavelengths, I wear out the dial on the radio switching from one program to another, in case I should miss my "Bing time." I worry over his publicity, note whether he gets top billing, etc. I would rather hear Bing sing not too well than hear anybody else sing superlatively. I enjoy a Crosby musical flop better than anyone else's hit. I love the sound of his speaking voice.

When I read that Mr. Crosby is standoffish to pressmen I defend him; some call him lazy but I admire his unwillingness to be pushed around. In the same way that Sinatra causes teen-age "bobby-soxers" to swoon, so Bing produces a comparable although less drastic effect on me. I don't pass out, but I feel completely limp when I hear him. . . . His voice makes me happy so that I smile and feel I want to laugh out loud. When I see Bing on the screen my heart thumps and I want desperately for everybody to like him.

Whether all that is love I don't know. . . . In spite of this fanaticism I have never written to Bing, asked for his autograph or collected his newspaper clippings, all because, I fear, I am too lazy. My pre-Bing screen favorite was Mickey Rooney. Whether I outgrew him, or whether

he outgrew his screen roles, I don't know. . . . My reasons
for liking him less were not caused by his marriages either.
The stars' private lives make no difference to their
performances on the screen.

age: 18   sex: female   nationality: British
profession: stenographer
. . . Then I went to see *The Adventures of Robin Hood* and
I promptly fell in love with Errol Flynn and rushed to
see his every film. I still have a number of the photos I
collected in the first flush of my crush on him. . . .
I interested myself in other stars. Rita Hayworth, Betty
Grable, and Alice Faye adorned my bedroom walls,
pushing out Errol Flynn and William Powell.

Every form of love, from the most naive to the most complex, and in every degree, can be found in these testimonials. Let us examine some others.

A gift of oneself, love is often accompanied by concrete
gifts that symbolize and consecrate it. There are several
kinds, from the "lay" present, a prestige item that implies
and entices a present in return, to the religious offering, a
humble gesture of piety that hopes for kindness and good-
will in return (a gift is rarely gratuitous), but first of all
seeks to gladden the idol's heart. Flowers, trinkets, curios,
lucky pieces, statuettes, sweaters, animals, dolls, and the like
are the offerings that constantly accumulate at the feet of
the stars.

Each week Luis Mariano expresses his thanks in *Cinémonde:*

Thanks to all my friends for the flowers, presents and
birthday wishes. (April 27, 1954)

A thousand thanks for the pretty blue sweater you sent me
just before I left on a trip. I was not able to use it in Mex-
ico, of course, but I was happy to wear it in Canada. It is
extremely warm. All my thanks again and my warmest

greetings, Odette. I hope to hear from you soon. (April 23, 1954)

My thanks to Violette for this original tobacco jar which reminds me of my trip through the mining country. And thank you, dear Lisa of Brussels, for your present which is as useful as it is original. Thank you, Odette, tardily, I'm afraid, for your cards from Nantes. . . . Thanks again to Monique S. of Lilas for her gift to our friends of St.-Fargeau. (October 27, 1955)

Marcella—I have received the two splendid volumes of the *History of Art*, for which I thank you with all my heart. But . . . to be honest, I should tell you that I had just bought them myself. Do you think you can exchange them at your bookstore? Perhaps if you know your bookseller well! (January 29, 1954)

Marie Antoinette—Mama and Maria Luisa were extremely touched by your presents and thank you affectionately, as do I.

Juanita de Alaya—Congratulations on your pretty photographs: especially the ones in the bathing suit, in gypsy costume, in the Mexican hat with your two cats, Figaro and Tchi-Ti-Kin, and the one in the charming dress at the gateway to my farm in Sare. All my congratulations on your success as a cameraman.

First of all, thanks to Edith Baugert for her friendly cards; to La Belle Louise for her cards from Notre Dame and for the bell, as well as for the delightful dolls from her collection; best wishes to Paula: thank you for the lovely dog and happy birthday too; the kitten from Rachel Eglesias is charming.

Martha—Thank you for your statuette of the Madonna and for the extremely lovely photograph of you.

Genevieve of Bordeaux—Thank you for your medal of St. Anthony of Padua.

Thank you for the lovely flowers.

Thank you for the splendid flowers that were waiting for me at Le Vesinet.

Thank you too for the rose petal symbolizing a whole bouquet and for the friendship that accompanies it.

Thank you for the lucky pieces and also for your caress inspired by my mustache. . . . Hola! (December 24, 1954)

Presents destined for the star's body (sweaters, food), symbolic or fetishistic presents (petals, dolls) suggest the gifts of natural substances and the symbolic offerings that mingle at the foot of the altars while the incense of praise smokes on high. One can even discern vestiges of a human sacrifice in the sixteen-year-old girl who offered Norma Shearer pieces of skin clipped from her own body.

As in every cult, the believer wants his god to hear him and respond. The stars receive by mail many confidences—sentimental, familial, and professional secrets. Some correspondents continue these interrupted confessions at regular intervals, presenting their lives in weekly slices to the star's magnanimous attention. In return the star must provide consolation or counsel, if not aid and protection. Some ask the stars, who appear generous on the screen, for work, money, old clothes.

At this point the star becomes identified with and ultimately transcends her screen image: by assimilating the moral virtues of every movie heroine she becomes analogous to the tutelary saints, to the guardian angels. "Joan Crawford is my lucky star. I feel she is near me, like a goddess, in my darkest hours" (from a young girl's letter).[3] The star is consulted on every imaginable problem, ordinary or extraordinary, and his responses guide the believers along the thorny paths of life. Luis Mariano's correspondence reveals him as an eminent spiritual guide who knows how to combine concrete hygienic or even alimentary advice with moral observation and metaphysical precept:

Cellou—if I have been able, even without knowing it, to relieve your unhappiness a little, I am glad. But I should prefer you to moderate this overviolent feeling a little and feel for me only the brotherly friendship which I have for you. Keep your spirits up and try harder. . . . Happiness is everywhere and calmly waits for us at the rendezvous of every hour. You will never find it in images and illusions. (*Cinémonde*, December 17, 1954)

Andre Rodrigue—The only way to become a good singer is to work hard with good teachers. (December 21, 1954)

Madame Nguien Dinh-Thoi—I am not sure how to advise you. You must decide for yourself whether you will eventually return to Indo-China with your husband. As for the *solfège* lessons, it is always good for children to come in contact early with music that will later bring them joy and consolation even if they do not use it professionally. (February 11, 1955)

And I am sure you can write short stories, even long ones. Novels will come later. In any case, I am looking forward to your first work. Write again. (December 3, 1954)

I would advise a young girl not to go into the movies. . . . For there are more than a thousand of you each month, in France alone, who have had the same idea, and the movies are not an easy life. (February 11, 1953)

Lilian Troarn—You are right, little sister, an actor's life is very hard; but keep your courage up and in a few years we will talk about it in all seriousness. (December 3, 1954)

Andre Donald—You too would like to be in the movies. . . . You think you can follow the stars' postmen and get inside the studio doors, but it is not so easy as all that. Nevertheless, with a lot of determination and a little talent you should get somewhere. First of all, take courses in acting and diction as well; they are indispensable. (March 18, 1955)

On occasion the star expresses a few thoughts on human nature:

> I do not have preferences. For me, a woman should be sentimental, pretty without too much affectation, simple, fond of children and her home, and—especially—must be spic and span . . . not to say clean . . . as you point out so well yourself. (Luis Mariano in *Cinémonde*, May 10, 1955)

> Why not choose a less dangerous profession? For a woman a certain degree of femininity is still indispensable, believe me. Men esteem strong women, but in general marry the ones with a childlike nature. (May 10, 1955)

> I close by recommending that you do not confuse frankness with politeness. (April 6, 1955)

> We must all move with the times. (April 6, 1955)

> Do not confuse draughtsmanship with spontaneous genius. Of course, after two years of school or at least of courses, you should be able to make your way to a splendid career as well as anyone else. But painting sometimes requires gifts; draughtsmanship requires only talent, patience, and taste. (February 11, 1955)

> Yes, in life you must have the determination to succeed: what the weak call stubborness.

> As for your diet, if you eat only wholesome, well-prepared food you have nothing to worry about. (December 24, 1954)

The star knows the secret of great consolations.

> Josette of Marseilles—Dear child of the land of sunshine, don't be sad. Of course there are books left . . . my books: write me and I will answer you. Of course I can dedicate them to you. At present, it's easier because I am in Paris and although I am extremely busy, I will save you a few minutes. Do you feel better? (December 8, 1955)

The supreme advice: the star urges his worshippers not to adore him too much.

> Paris—Madrid—A marble and gold monument to be set up in the Place de la Concorde? Now don't be disappointed, but my friends in the Club have better things to do than spend their money on a statue to me. Think of some other idea and don't be angry. (March 25, 1955)

> Look around you and meditate on what you see. "Go out, live, what does it matter!"—that has never been one of my mottoes. Do not behave like some girls: do not regard every boy you meet with either disgust or love. The day when you will really be in love you will only realize it by how much you miss the very person to whom you had not even given a thought . . . that boy with the gentle look, that friend at work who is so considerate and so far from your mind? Believe me, as its name indicates, love at first sight does not last, and life is made up of many hours. (February 18, 1955)

> A Tearful Heart—(that's really too sad). 1. Why not? 2. Yes, they say God makes those who love suffer, so console yourself, you will be rewarded for your trials, all the more because I believe they are imaginary. You will understand later, alas! that true suffering is different from this melancholy you are amusing yourself with because you have spent too much time on it. . . . Do something, no matter what: work, sports, charity. But give no more time to this "unrealizable dream." (September 11, 1953)

To inflamed declarations, Luis Mariano fraternally replies:

> With no hard feelings and a big kiss from your new big brother. (April 6, 1955)

> Write me again; I embrace you like a big brother, which I am—doubtless—and until then. (February 18, 1955)

But this friendly sincerity merely increases the star's mythic prestige: his noble disinterest, brotherly affection, and exquisite simplicity bear witness to his profound humanity and greatness of soul. Modesty always plays a part in the myth of greatness.

The star is like a patron saint to whom the faithful dedicate themselves, but who must also to a certain degree dedicate himself to the faithful. Furthermore, the worshipper always desires to *consume* his god. From the cannibal repasts in which the ancestor was eaten, and the totemic feasts in which the sacred animal was devoured, down to our own religious communion and receiving of the Eucharist, every god is created to be eaten—that is, incorporated, assimilated. Information is the first stage of this assimilation. The faithful want to know everything: possess, manipulate, and mentally digest the total image of the idol. Information is one means of magic appropriation. It does not tend to constitute an analytic or synthetic body of knowledge about the star, but to snap up gossip, rumors, indiscretions in a delectable englutting.

Hence the enormous quantity of Hollywood and other cinema gossip columns. These columns are not the by-products but the nutritive plankton of the star system. The journalists of the cinema are more interested in the stars than in the films, and more interested in gossip about the stars than in the stars. They smell out, track down, and kidnap rumors and, if need be, invent them. The information services and gossip columns have as their function not only the transformation of real life into myth and of myth into reality: they must get to the bottom of everything and offer what they have unearthed to an insatiable curiosity.

Beauty secrets, cosmetic, dietary, or aesthetic preferences, travels, expenses, furniture, pets—all intimate details are material for the columns. Hence we are gratified by articles such as "Why I Like Fried Potatoes," by Ginger Rogers, and "A Husband Should Be Made to Shave," by Hedy Lamarr. The dark curls of Luis Mariano no longer hold any secrets for us:

I have my hair cut off so that it will grow in thicker.
(*Cinémonde*, February 11, 1955)

No, I don't use lotions, but I brush my hair very regularly,
and recently I had it cut very short so it would grow in
thicker. (December 24, 1954)

His aesthetic preferences, too, are revealed:

I like every color of hair; country girls are lighthearted
and lovely. (December 3, 1954)

My favorite reading . . . Recently I have re-read with
pleasure the works of Julien Green, Jean Giono, and de
Montherlant . . . whenever I have a minute on a train, a
boat, or a plane. (December 3, 1954)

All such information whispers some little secret that will
permit the reader to gain possession of a morsel of intimacy
with the star. This morsel can eventually be utilized by each
fan, who adopts hairstyles, makeup, styles of dress, and
assimilates the assimilable material par excellence, the star's
favorite food. Hence the importance in these confessions,
indiscretions, and interviews of what the godless consider
worthless details.

Like every spontaneous and naive cult that is supported
by those who profit from it, the cult of the stars has blos-
somed into fetishism. Impotent love attempts to fix itself
on a fragment, a symbol of the beloved in default of her real
presence.

The gossip column satisfies one requirement of fetishistic knowledge: the star's weight, her favorite dishes, the brand
of her underwear, her hip measurements, are all presence-
bearers, endowed with the precision and the objectivity of
the real in the absence of reality itself. The same requirement attaches concretely to photographs, the universal
presence-fetishes of the twentieth century. The photograph
is the best ersatz of the real presence: permanent alter ego,

a minor presence, whether in pocket or apartment, radiant and instructive, it can be contemplated and adored. Hence about 90 percent of all fan letters ask for photographs.

Photographs are accumulated and exchanged, treasured and compared. What is there that cannot be confessed to a photograph? What is there it cannot reply? The autograph completes the photograph with a direct, concrete, personal imprint. Ninety percent of all fan letters ask for autographs as well, or rather ask for a photograph inscribed with an autograph—a line in which the star expresses her tutelary benevolence: "Lovingly yours," "With all my heart," "In friendship."

The autograph is not always or only written on note-book paper. "At the premiere of *Anna and the King of Siam*, two girls between seventeen and eighteen years old broke through the barricades, threw themselves on Van Johnson, lifted their skirts over their heads, and asked their idol to autograph their panties."[4]

Photographs and autographs are the two key fetishes, to which are added collections of clippings (materialization of the gossip column fetishes), handkerchiefs, locks of hair, and so on. After the release of one of Dorothy Lamour's films, Paramount received in a few days more than six thousand letters asking for a lock of the star's hair.[5] Finally, every possible and imaginable object that contact with the star has made radioactive can become a fetish: cigarette butts, used chewing gum, buttons, grass sanctified by the star's foot, shoelaces, pieces of cloth.

Leo Rosten has cataloged several of the fetishist requests and offers addressed to two Hollywood stars in January 1939:

soap
fur
used cosmetic tissue
a banjo

a spoon
salt and pepper shakers
used chewing gum
a bicycle
three hairs
hairpins
a sock or stocking
a wristwatch
pearls
dress, hat, and shoes
handkerchiefs
an offer to mortgage the writer's life or services for a
    certain amount of money
a telegram to a cousin on his birthday
matchbox cover
aviator's helmet
hair from the star's horse's tail or mane
a sales order with three carbons from a department store
an offer to say prayers
cigarette butts
eleven pages with "I love you" written 825 times on each
    one
a coat button
a note saying "Wait for me."
a tame flea named after the star
a million dollars in movie money
a pair of autographed undershorts
a collar button
an offer to take the place of the star's dog
a blade of grass from the star's lawn

Like primitive man confronted with a god who has not
answered his prayers, the fans overwhelm the stars with
reproaches when they fail in their duties to respond, advise,
console. One letter addressed to Robert Taylor so exem-
plarily formulated the worshippers' quivering rebellion that

it was published by a magazine, which awarded it a prize of one dollar:

> I think you should pay more attention to the letters your fans send you. If you neglect doing this, you are going to lose a lot of your fans. The first time I saw you in the movies I wrote you a letter; I never received an answer. I have since written you three letters; I have never had an answer to any of them. On your birthday I sent you a pretty birthday card for which you never thanked me. Do you think you should treat your fans this way? Put yourself in my place, and imagine what your feelings would be if you never heard from someone you liked so much.[6]

The worshipper can also protest when his idol lays violent hands on his own image. Thus Bing Crosby's fans complained at seeing him drunk in *Sing You Sinners.* When Jean-Claude Pascal's fans found themselves unable to tolerate his becoming blond, Jean-Claude Pascal turned brunette again. In this reference, mustache problems are even more serious and give rise to passionate polemics. Should Dick Powell or Luis Mariano wear a mustache or not? The star cannot decide such a thorny question by himself and entrusts the verdict to his admirers:

> But do you really prefer me with a mustache? I am making a little survey at present . . . for or against. (Luis Mariano, *Cinémonde*, October 1954)

The faithful supervise the mustache and the hairstyles of their idol. Each of them, of course, would like to control everything else as well and exclusively. Only the youngest and maddest dare express this dream:

> "I am thirteen years old and would like to marry you," writes one, at the age of illusion (Luis Mariano's mail, *Cinémonde*, 25-2-55). Once the illusions collapse, a bronze statue will do. The case of one Irish boy who at the age of

twenty-eight still cherished hopes of going to Hollywood
to marry Deanna Durbin is exceptional.[7]

If the faithful sometimes cannot keep from revealing their
inmost dreams, they are nevertheless aware of the impossibility of them. As Luis Mariano philosophically concludes,
"Dream away: I am nothing more for you than a substitute
for your teddy bear."

The cult of the stars reveals its profoundest meaning at
certain moments of collective hysteria, such as those provoked by the death of Valentino or James Dean, the arrival
of Lollobrigida at Cannes or of Sophia Loren in Paris, and
other revolutionary events. Dekeukeleire cites the example of
certain citizens of Brussels who, in 1928, "kissed the tires
of Henri Garat's car, reminding us of the annual procession of
the sacred cart at Benares."[8] In Hollywood, a flock of girls
often rushes upon a star, pulls at her hair, and rips off her
coat or even her dress in frenzy.

We can now discern one of the fundamental characteristics
of the cult of the stars. Mental, mystical, fetishist appropriation, assimilation, and consumption are all various modes
of identification. Like every spectacle, although more viv-
idly, the spectacle of the movies implies a process of psychic
identification of the spectator with the action represented.
The spectator psychically lives the exciting, intense, amorous,
imaginary life of the movie heroes—that is, identifies himself with them.

This identification functions in two directions: the first
is the amorous projection-identification addressed to a partner of the opposite sex, Rudolph Valentino, Bing Crosby,
Luis Mariano, or Greta Garbo, Lucia Bose, Grace Kelly.
The second, more widespread today, is an identification
with an alter ego, that is, a star of the same sex and the same
age. As all investigations made on this subject reveal, boys
tend to prefer male stars, girls female stars.[9] The age of the

worshippers often corresponds to the star's age. Leo Rosten notes that *the letters addressed to a young star are written for the most part by young fans, whereas the older fans write to "middle-aged" stars*. Finally, regional preferences (Fernandel in Marseilles, "western" stars in the Rocky Mountains) indicate in their turn that identities not only of age and sex but also of origin permit, accelerate, or amplify the identification process. Furthermore, the admirers of the stars are very often conscious of this process.[10]

Why do you prefer this star?	
Identification	35
Affinity, sympathy	27
Actors of this sex act better	22
Idealization, idolatry	10
Admiration of manners, style, etc.	4

The identification generated in the movie theater can persist beyond the spectacle in daydreams: "I have always made up stories (with myself as the heroine) based on the movies I see and the heroes I love" (English schoolgirl of fifteen). "When I came back home I dreamed I was the beautiful leading lady in a magnificent crinoline, with a feather in my hair" (apprentice hairdresser of sixteen).[11]

But this dream borders on and even collides with reality. The spectator feels very small and very much alone and sees the star as very large and majestic. He becomes a worshipper of what he would like to be. According to the star's type, as we shall see further on, the worshipper can feel himself so humble that he no longer even dares to identify himself with the star. He may also wish to continue his dream, and thus seeks mystic aids to identification: autographs, photographs, fetishes, gossip columns, symbols of real presence, subjects of mythical presence—all are so many exterior means for living the life of the stars mystically and from within. The sympathetic magic functions either in a totally oneiric fashion or in an oneiric-practical way: in the latter case, the adorer comes to imitate unconsciously or consciously some aspect of the idol.

To this total oneiric imitation (the dream in which identification with the star is complete) corresponds an atrophied practical mimetism: the fan follows the star's dietary and bodily practice, adopts her makeup, imitates her clothes, her manners, her mannerisms: "I did my hair as much like hers as I could. . . . I found myself wondering what Deanna would do."

> When I was seventeen I saw a star about whom the boy I was with said: "She has the most lovely little feet and her shoes are always beautiful." I had nice feet and made a vow that the same should be said of me. I don't know if it ever was, but I always bought the nicest shoes and stockings I could afford and shoes are still my pet luxury, even in these days of rationing." (British secretary, thirty-nine years old)[12]

> I remember having copied the style of a dress worn by Myrna Loy in a film and feeling very "Hollywood" whenever I wore it. (secretary, twenty-three years old)

> The settings of the love scenes always held my attention and I've always noted little tricks (which I've put into practice) such as curling my boyfriend's hair in my fingers or stroking his face exactly as I've seen my screen favorites do in their love scenes. One of the first things I noticed was that an actress always closes her eyes when being kissed and I don't need to add that I copied that too. (girl, nineteen years old)

Movie advertising even organizes great identification contests: the Helen of Troy contest (identification with Rossana Podesta), the Romeo and Juliet contest.

The religion of the stars is precisely that imaginary practice that permits the identification-producing dialectic of fan and star. The same cult includes an adoring love of both heterosexual and homosexual characteristics. This is because both imply the same transformation of the star into the fan's alter ego and even of the fan into the star's alter ego. It is because, even as all self-love conquers love of others, in an individualist civilization like ours, in which love is also egoism, all love of others implies self-love. The same word, *love*, we have seen, intervenes in both forms of adoration. A schoolboy of fifteen writes quite naturally: "My film idol is Errol Flynn and I fell madly in love with him after seeing *Dawn Patrol*. I think about him at night, pretend I am with him, and dream about him. I have never felt about a film actress in this way."

Participation is not only identification of the spectator with the hero. In the last analysis it is neither talent nor lack of talent, neither the cinematic industry nor its advertising, but the *need* for her that creates a star. It is the misery of need, the mean and anonymous life that wants to enlarge itself to the dimensions of life in the movies. The imaginary life of the screen is the product of this genuine need; the star is its projection.

Man has always projected his desires and his fears in images. He has always projected in his own image—his double—his need to transcend himself in life and in death. This double is the repository of latent magical powers; every double is a virtual god.

The objects and persons of the screen universe are images, doubles; the actor's role as hero divides him into two beings; the projection of the spectator onto the hero corresponds to a doubling action: these triple doublings, as one may call them, promote the mythic ferment. Their combination brings the star into being by investing the real actor with magic potentialities. Beyond the image, the mythic projections focus on the concrete and actual person: the star. Given strength by her double, of course, she invests her double in her turn: the star is plunged into the mirror of dreams and brought back into view on the level of tangible reality. In both directions *she is affected only by the powers of projection, which divinize her*. It is when the mythic *projection* focuses on her double nature and unifies it that the star-goddess is produced. But this goddess must be consumed, assimilated, integrated: the cult is organized to accomplish this *identification*. The star is the product of a projection-identification complex of a particular virulence.

The movies, machines for doubling life, summon the heroic and amorous myths to incarnation on the screen, start again the old imaginary processes of identification and projection from which gods are born. The religion of the stars crystallizes the projection-identification inherent in all participation in the film.

According to the virulence of either projection or identification, two major types of gods may be distinguished: father-gods and son-gods (heroes or demigods). The "father" is so remote and grandiose a projection of human terrors and ambitions that his worshippers dare not identify themselves with him except in their most secret dreams. The cult of the great transcendent gods comprises only a few very weak identification practices. On the other hand, the bastard hero-god, the son of man, is the very subject of the lived identification; he brings man salvation, that is, the means to accede to the condition of the gods: immortality. The believer must imitate—it is sufficient that he imitate—the hero-god's passion, mystically living his sacrifice, in order to acquire the divine immortality.

The star system knows or rather has known historically, mutatis mutandis, both these stages of adoration. At the supreme, inaccessible level, the "divine" star; here adoration does not yet imply mimetism, either because the star keeps herself at an unvarying distance or because the believer merely feels too humble even to hope to be able to imitate her. As one stenographer already quoted puts it: "I admired Norma Talmadge and Mary Pickford, and I thought a lot about them, but I have never hoped to resemble them or do what they did." But more often, the star hovers at the level of the divinized hero who can be identified with oneself, with whom one can identify, and who contributes to the personal salvation of each devotee.

For the great majority of spectators, of course, the star's divinity is embryonic. Yet personal preferences, emotions, reveries, tender and admiring feelings excite certain religiosity. If this sentiment is not yet a religion, it contains its seed. It is actually at the very point where this sentiment ferments, candidly and fervently—among adolescents and among women—that the star's divinity blossoms.

According to Leo Rosten and Margaret Thorp, 75 to 90 percent of the fans are less than twenty-one years old, and approximately 80 percent are of the female sex, whatever the sex of the star. This feminine preponderance gives the star system a feminine character. "Mythification" is effected primarily upon female stars: they are the most "fabricated," the most idealized, the least real, the most adored. In present-day social conditions, woman is more mythic than man as both subject and object. She is naturally more of a star than a man. That is why we have generally referred to the star as "she." We have naturally feminized the star; in French the word *star* itself is feminine.

Female stars are the object of a masculine attraction and of a feminine cult. Male stars are the object of a feminine cult. This does not mean that men take no interest in male stars. The investigations reported above (by the Motion Picture Research Bureau and by Gallup in 1941) reveal that preference for stars of one's own sex is more pronounced among men than among women. But if they are more numerous, masculine identifications are less mystical. For a man the star is less a sacred archetype than a profane *model:* he imitates the male star but does not wish to know him. He prefers him, but without revering him.

Love and admiration for the stars are concretized into a religion for only a section of the public. This religion is fragile and subject to disintegration. There comes the moment when the star grows old and dies. There comes the moment when the fan, too, grows old: real life erodes admiration, a real lover substitutes for the star. The star's divinity is ephemeral. Time erodes it, and it escapes only in memory. Death is stronger than immortality. *But this very fragility reveals the force of the religious sentiment that has come to flower.* The star is divinized in spite of her evident "humanity," in spite of her submission to the outrages of time, in spite of the aesthetic consciousness of the spectator, who knows that the star is playing a role in the cinema and not living a passion.

Nevertheless, the star straddles both sacred and profane, divine and real, aesthetic and magic, like the kings. "O kings, you are gods," exclaimed Bossuet. O stars, you are queens. Accession to the throne is already a divinization, tyrants and emperors already "blessed" and "august." The star and the king are flesh-and-blood creatures infected by their roles. The same mythology envelops their person, penetrates it, determines it. The same public confidence surrounds their private life; the same life of luxury, ceremony, and spectacle, a life of dream-reality, is imposed on them. We admire them without envying them; we are not jealous of kings or of stars.

Furthermore, the twentieth century, which makes royalty of the stars, makes stars of its kings. The latter occupy the same place, the same role as the stars in *Paris-Match* and *France-Dimanche*. The romance of Princess Margaret and Peter Townsend, a "real-life film," immediately inspired a film, *Roman Holiday*. The marriage of Grace Kelly and Prince Rainier in reality, *Royal Affairs in Versailles* in fiction, consecrate the mythic analogy of the king and the star; when each king, each prince, each illustrious personage is incarnated by a star, Sacha Guitry can reconstitute the historic grandeur of France.

The king derives his prestige from political power. The star, on the other hand, is an aesthetic product, that is, the result not of belief, but of play. Nevertheless, she is situated at that point where the aesthetic, in its élan and its persuasive force, transcends itself to recover the primitive vigor of its magic source. The star is on the border between the aesthetic and magic. She overcomes the skepticism of the spectator-consciousness, which always knows that it is participating in an illusion.

Of course the spectator knows that the star is human and, even more precisely, an actress making a movie; of course the institutions of the cult of the stars, in spite of their evident mystical character, remain profane: clubs, magazines, correspondence, presents, and not temple, bible, litanies, offerings; yet all the processes of divinization are in action beneath these lay forms, and it is these processes that characterize the star. Parker Tyler expresses it perfectly: "Anthropomorphic gods—the term must not be taken literally, but it is not merely a manner of speaking."

The star is made from a substance compounded of life and dream. She incarnates herself in the archetypes of the universe of fiction. But the heroes of novels, ectoplasmic and inconsistent, incarnate themselves in the archetype of the star. Model and imitator, exterior to the film and at its heart, determining it but determined by it, the star is a syncretic personality in which the real person cannot be distinguished

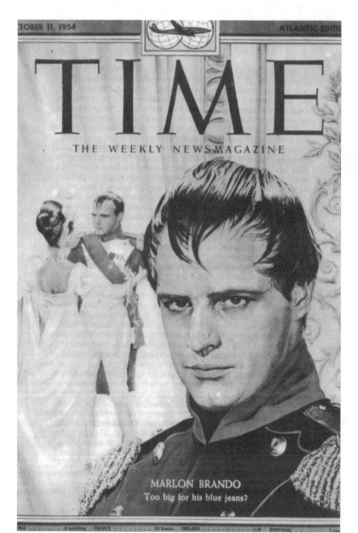

OCTOBER 11, 1954   ATLANTIC EDITION

TIME

THE WEEKLY NEWSMAGAZINE

MARLON BRANDO
Too big for his blue jeans?

from the person fabricated by the dream factories and the person invented by the spectator. Her mythic power changed into real power that can modify films and scenarios and direct the destiny of her admirers, *the star is of the same double nature as the heroes of mythologies—mortals aspiring to immortality, candidates for divinity, tutelary spirits, half-men, half-gods.* During the film, these heroes and these heroines struggle, suffer, remedy, redeem. Off the screen, the stars lead the Elysian life of pleasures and play reserved for heroes after their death.

Hero, demigod, René Clair has already said as much in his novel *Adam's:* "The men of the enlightenment salute the demigods they have given themselves. . . . The measureless bodies of these demigods dominate the world. . . . Love and the aging world had need of adorable faces . . . for these the mystical applause, the gaze inspired by supernatural love."[13]

Nonsense, no doubt! Nonsense from which the serious sociologist turns away in disgust, which is why no one has yet dared to study the stars. But our scholars betray their frivolity in their refusal to take nonsense seriously. Nonsense is *also* what is most profound in man. Behind the star system there is not only the "stupidity" of fanatics, the lack of invention of screenwriters, the commercial chicanery of producers. There is the world's heart and there is love, another kind of nonsense, another profound humanity.

There is also that magic we regard as the characteristic of "primitives" and that is at the very heart of our civilized lives. The old magic is still there. Every village in France is dominated by a bell tower, but in the back rooms of cafés in these very villages, in the barns and garages of the common adoration, in the cities, wherever there is a white screen in a black room, a new religion has been established. And what is more, in each of our hearts, the religion of love rules, all-powerful. The star system derives from the old religion of immortality and from the new, all-powerful religion of a mortal scale: love.

Rationalist Europe and rationalizing America, religious and amorous, brandish their colossal carnival dolls, their stars. Let us look for new scholars who will know how to describe the ethnography of nonprimitive societies. Your turn, Africans, Oceanians, Amerindians, objects and victims of ethnography! And do not be merely disdainful collectors as we have been in regard to you.

The stars are like the gods: everything and nothing. The divine substance that fills and crowds this nothingness is human love. The god's infinite void is also an infinite richness, but it is a richness not his own. The star is empty of all divinity, as are the gods. The star is full of all humanity, as are the gods.

The Chaplin Mystery

The star is the product of a dialectic of personality: an actor imposes his personality on the heroes he plays, these heroes impose their personality on the actor. From this superimpression is born a composite being: the star. The actor contributes the capital of his own personality: we have seen, in the case of the female star, that beauty can be an ultimately necessary and sufficient support of this personality, and furthermore that beauty, like personality, can be manufactured.

Unlike feminine beauty, masculine beauty does not depend on makeup, hairstyles, surgery, and so on. It is less frequently determined by delicacy, regularity, or harmony of features. On the other hand, whereas the personality of the female star is almost entirely a function of an erotic archetype, the personality of the male star is much more closely related to qualities that are actually heroic: the masculine hero does battle not only for his love but against wickedness, destiny, injustice, death.

In either case, male and female stars possess the primary qualities from which the processes of idealization and divinization develop by nature. But these primary qualities are lacking in one special category of stars, and not the most negligible—the comic stars. The heroes they incarnate—ugly, timid, boastful, ridiculous—are the contrary of the hero proper. Nevertheless, on a scale entirely different, of course, from that of the romantic stars, the comic stars too are "idols of crowds." Among them was born the greatest of all stars, so great that he exploded the star system: Charlie Chaplin.

How can buffoons, ridiculous clowns, anti-idols, be idolized? How does the personality of comic stars impose itself on the crowd? The comic heroes are apparently the negatives of actual heroes. The comic stars are apparently the caricatures of the stars of romance and heroism. But perhaps despite these evident oppositions, both genres derive their powers from the same mythic source.

The comic stars are the result of one of the most original genres of movie history, a genre that flourished from 1912–14 (1912: Mack Sennett's first comedy, *Cohen at Coney Island*) to the beginnings of the talkies. After the period of slapstick comedy, the comic heroes have survived more or less successfully in the Fernandels, Danny Kayes, Bourvils, and so on.

The comic heroes of slapstick comedy are obviously those who receive more kicks in the pants, knocks on the head, and custard pies in the face than they deal out: they are essentially persecuted men. The world actually does persecute them. Every possible misfortune happens to them. They attract bad luck, which then seems to adhere to them. We would feel pity and grief for their sufferings if, of course, we were not laughing so hard.

The comic heroes are bewildered, naive, or idiotic. At least apparently, for their stupidity has no other function than to express their fundamental innocence. A quasi-infantile innocence, which is the basis of their intimacy with children (*The Kid*).

The comic hero is an innocent who does not understand what is happening. He thinks he sees good where there is evil, salvation where there is perdition (compare the theme of the gangster-in-spite-of-himself). An innocent who obeys his immediate impulses, he rushes at food on a table, caresses everything that seems pretty to him, translates all his desires into acts. He meddles with everything that is forbidden. As Enrico Piceni puts it, "We obey our conscious mind; Chaplin obeys his subconscious."[1]

Thus the comic hero stumbles roughshod over all the little taboos of social life. He flicks cigarette ashes into the front of a lady's gown, walks on her train, and so on. Better still: the comic hero violates the taboos of property (he steals) and of religion (he disguises himself as a preacher and officiates at a service), which sets him beyond rules, outside the law. Chaplin the tramp, forever pursued by policemen, is, like all the great movie heroes, but in his own ludicrous way, an outlaw.

The comic hero is unaware of censure and reproof. His childish innocence impels him as much toward abnormal kindness as toward abnormal mischief. He is good because he expresses all his good impulses, but he is also amoral. Chaplin always steals without scruples; he is even innocently cruel, and delights in hitting the aching leg of an invalid paralyzed by gout.

Monsieur Verdoux, who ceases to be a hero of slapstick comedy, merely develops these virtualities: he realizes his murderous impulses in completely innocent amorality (like the hero of *Noblesse Oblige*). Full of kindness, affection, devotion for those he loves, he assassinates with nonchalant lack of guile those who offend him.

The comic hero is also a sexual innocent, as both Leites and Tyler have pointed out. He lacks the psychological characteristics of virility (courage, decision, boldness with women) and often manifests signs of effeminacy. Threatened by formidable bullies, all he can do is smirk and simper (Chaplin, Fatty Arbuckle).

Chaplin, when terrified, hysterically indicates a thousand

seductive gestures, wriggling, pouting (reciprocally the comic heroine is preferably phallic, the sex-hungry female: Betty Hutton). The comic hero is always awkward with the girl: he does not dare kiss her, not even when she offers him her lips.

All the same, this desexualized hero is frequently in love. His love is sublime because it is not founded on sexual domination and appropriation: it is a total gift of himself, like infantile or canine love.

The comic hero, in fact, following his impulses, behaves like a somnambulist. The face of Buster Keaton, Chaplin's mechanical gait, betray a "possession" that is quasi-hypnotic. This possession, which makes them commit every possible blunder, can also lead them to final triumph. By blundering, by his blunders themselves, the comic hero can vanquish his enemies and even seduce the woman he loves. Thus Bourvil in *Le trou normand* tries to fail his graduation exam, and at the question, "Who was the wife of Louis XVI?" having decided it was Catherine de Médicis, answers, "Marie Antoinette!"

The comic hero always finds himself in the same situations, always assumes the same roles. In this sense, he is still

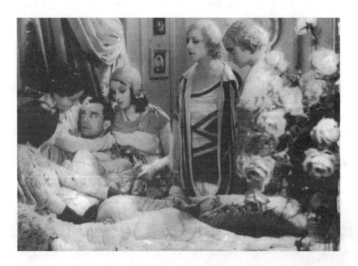

closely related to the fools, buffoons, and clowns of whom he is the heir, but he is just as closely related to the inno-cent martyrs, little match girls, abandoned orphans, and molested virgins of the melodramas. *His innocence dedicates him to the purifying role of a drudge and a butt, but on the scale of the ludicrous.* In the last analysis, he plays the quasi-sacred role of the purifying victim and the scapegoat. The most effec-tive victims are the most innocent; the comic hero is inno-cent, like Isaac, Iphigenia, the mystic Lamb. He is the butt of every blow and every insult. He suffers permanently for everyone else. His tortures provoke laughter, which is as liberating as tears, or more so. Subject to a possession that transcends him, the comic hero represents not the profane but the negative of the sacred, the profaned.

The comic hero is thus a variant of the sacrificial hero, the redeeming martyr. Furthermore, if his tragic aspects are ridiculous, his ridiculous aspects can become tragic, can even imply a permanent tragedy. Hence the frequent theme of "laugh, clown, laugh"—the clown who screams his laughter in order to conceal his sobs. This theme exposes our obscure awareness of the profoundly painful role that

buffoons and clowns assume. Furthermore, the Chaplins, Fernandels, Raimus easily become the most touching of movie actors: those who know how to make us laugh until we cry know best how to make us cry.

The comic hero is indeed a hero in the full sense of the term. Hence the comic star is possible, not only because the actor is infected by his role at the same time that his personal genius determines this role (much more strongly than other movie roles are determined) but because his personality is endowed with the sacrificial function of the comic hero.

This particular divinization that constantly dissolves into profane laughter is as constantly rebuilt in the immolation of the scapegoat. No matter how remote the comic hero may seem from deification, he approaches it in a dialectical fashion. Charlie Chaplin is the great example: since the twenties, Chaplin's genius has revealed the simultaneously ludicrous and painful aspects of "the tramp." The whole evolution from Charlie the tramp to Calvero will form an increasingly conscious exploration of a sacrificial character apprehended at its veritable human source.

By nature the comic film ignores not, of course, the corpse, the skeleton, or the ghost, but death. Furthermore, in the course of its evolution and for reasons we have already indicated, it is oriented toward the happy ending, that is, the final sleight of hand that masks the hero's self-sacrifice. Chaplin, on the contrary, with the exception of *Modern Times*, binds himself to the logical meaning of this sacrifice: to give way to someone else, to be abandoned by the girl he loves, and finally to die.

In another respect, and in part under Chaplin's influence, the comic hero acquires a chivalric character. In the precinematic tradition the clown is opposed to the knight (Sancho Panza and Don Quixote). The cinema, involving a massive phenomenon of democratization, tends to transfer the comic hero to a knightly role. Chaplin continues the tradition of the clown, the slave trembling in terror of his own shadow; yet, when love requires it, he is the defender and even the savior of threatened beauty. As Parker Tyler points out, Chaplin is a curious melange of Don Quixote and Sancho Panza. Danny Kaye, Fernandel, and so on, are also chivalrous despite their buffoonery. But Chaplin, in assuming the knight's role, tends to transform himself from a purifier into a redeemer. Instead of a scapegoat, he becomes a love god who sacrifices himself for others.

Because of love and for love's sake, Chaplin will accept and ultimately seek self-sacrifice. From Charlie the tramp to Calvero, the development to the point of self-immolation is implacably traced. As far back as *The Circus*, Chaplin self-effacingly stood aside, yielding to others a happiness acquired through his own efforts. In *City Lights*, he lets himself be imprisoned, deprived of light and freedom, so the little blind girl can discover them. Chaplin naturally dedicates himself to the crippled, blind, or paralyzed woman, to the desperate girl, to the child, a social cripple. On each occasion, his sacrifice is expressed as a salvation, a *vita nuova*, a resurrection for someone else.

In *Monsieur Verdoux* for the first time appears the immolating fulfillment of the sacrifice: death. *Limelight* brings to a sublime climax the essential theme of redemption and self-sacrifice that retrospectively illuminates Verdoux's death, the tramp's solitude, and all the beatings submitted to by all of Chaplin's characters and by all clowns since the beginning of time.

Calvero could be happy with Terry. She tells him she loves him many times over, and he knows she does. She tries to keep him with her, but he answers, "I must follow my road; it's a law." He sacrifices himself voluntarily, consciously, in order to liberate youth and life from their chains. By means of buffoonery Calvero becomes a savior and a redeemer: "when the camera draws away from Calvero, dead in the wings, and rejoins on stage the ballerina dancing in spite of her despair, this movement of the machinery seems to

follow the very transference of souls" (André Bazin). We are concerned here with the transference appropriate to every sacrifice, the fecundation of life by death, by the total gift of oneself.

Thus Chaplin's evolution demonstrates in an almost exemplary way how the purifying scapegoat of slapstick comedy bears within itself the germs of the self-sacrificing hero, let us even say of the god who dies and redeems. Let us not hesitate to use the word *god*—Chaplin himself, five years ago, was planning a film that casts a final light on these notions: in a music hall the curtain rises on three crosses. The audience sees the Roman soldiers crucifying Jesus. Everyone applauds, but it was Jesus himself who was immolated. Charlie-Calvero, who makes the blind see and the paralytic walk, was already obscurely tending toward Jesus.

Thus the comic hero, too, is a version of the hero who takes evil upon himself in order to purify others. He possesses a virtual mythic and sacred power. We do not love him only because he makes us laugh; he makes us laugh so that we will love him.

Henceforth we understand why the comic should be one of the ways that leads to the heaven of the stars. But comic stardom has its own characteristics, determined by the ambivalence of the sacred and the profane, absurdity and pathos, love and scorn. The crowds of moviegoers love the comic hero, not amorously, but with a different fervor, one that is perhaps richer and more complex. Laughter is as strong, as profound, as beauty.

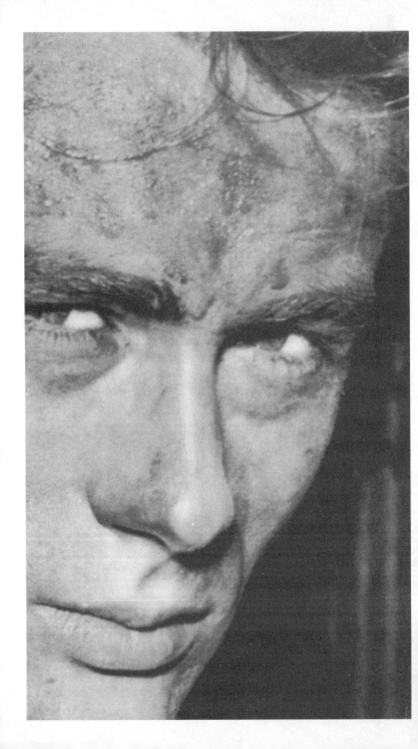

The Case of James Dean

The mythological hero is always abducted from his parents or the latter somehow are separated from him. James Dean was an orphan. His mother died when he was nine, and he was brought up by an uncle, a farmer in Fairmount.

The mythological hero must forge his own destiny in a struggle against the world. James Dean ran away from the university, worked as an icebreaker on a refrigeration truck, a stevedore on a tugboat, and a ship's boy on a yacht, until he assumed his place under the dazzling rays of our modern mythical sun: he appeared on the Broadway stage in *See the Jaguar*, then in *The Immoralist*. He went to Hollywood and made *East of Eden*.

The mythological hero undertakes many labors in which he proves his aptitudes and also expresses his aspiration toward the richest, most nearly total life possible. James Dean milked cows, tended chickens, drove a tractor, raised a bull, played star basketball, studied yoga and the clarinet, learned something about almost every field of knowledge, and finally became what in the modern world embodies the myth of total life: a movie star. James Dean wanted to do everything, to try everything, to experience everything. "If

I lived to be a hundred," he would say, "I still wouldn't have time to do everything I wanted."

The mythological hero aspires to the absolute, but cannot realize this absolute in a woman's love. James Dean would have had an unhappy life with Pier Angeli, who married Vic Damone: legend or reality? In any case, the legend is anchored in reality.

In front of the church that Pier Angeli left as a bride, James Dean gunned his motorcycle: the noise of the motor drowned out the sound of bells. Then he dragged violently and drove all the way to Fairmount, the cradle of his childhood. (We rediscover here the theme of the amorous failure, necessary to heroic accomplishment, as well as the theme of the feminine maleficence that every redeeming hero encounters.)

The mythological hero confronts more and more touchingly the world he desires to seize in its entirety. James Dean's destiny became increasingly breathless: he was obsessed by speed, the modern ersatz absolute. Seeming disturbed and feverish to some, extraordinarily serene to others, James Dean, after finishing *Giant*, drove off into the night at 160 miles an hour in his racing Porsche toward Salinas, where he was to enter an automobile race.

The mythological hero encounters death in his quest for the absolute. His death signifies that he is broken by the hostile forces of the world, but at the same time, in this very defeat, he ultimately gains the absolute: immortality. James Dean dies; it is the beginning of his victory over death.

The "heroic" life and character of James Dean are not prefabricated by the star system, but real, *revealed*. There is still more.

Heroes die young. Heroes are young. But our times have produced, in literature (Rimbaud, *The Wanderer*) and, decisively, in recent years, in the movies, heroes bearing the new message of adolescence. Since its origin, of course, the movies' greatest audience has been composed of adolescents. But it is only recently that adolescence has become conscious of itself as a particular age class, opposing itself to other age classes and defining its own imaginary range and cultural models.[1] Which is as clearly revealed in the novels of Françoise Sagan and Françoise Mallet-Joris as in the films of Marlon Brando and James Dean.

James Dean is a model, but this model is itself the typical expression (both average and pure) of adolescence in general and of American adolescence in particular. His face corresponds to a dominant physiognomic type, blond hair, regular features. Further, the mobility of his expressions admirably translates the double nature of the adolescent face, still hesitating between childhood's melancholy and the mask of the adult. The photogenic quality of this face, even more than that of Marlon Brando, is rich with all the indetermination of an ageless age, alternating scowls with astonishment, disarmed candor and playfulness with sudden hardness, resolution and rigor with collapse. Chin on chest, unexpectedly smiling, fluttering his eyelashes, mingling ostentation and reserve, being naive and gauche—that is, always sincere—the face of James Dean is an ever-changing landscape in which can be discerned the contradictions, uncertainties, and enthusiasms of the adolescent soul. It is understandable that this face should have become an insignia, that it is already imitated, especially in its most readily imitable features: hair and glance.

James Dean has also defined what one might call the panoply of adolescence, a wardrobe in which is expressed a whole attitude toward society: blue jeans, heavy sweaters, leather jacket, no tie, unbuttoned shirt, deliberate sloppiness are so many ostensible signs (having the value of political badges) of a resistance against the social conventions of a world of adults. Clothes are a quest for the signs of virility (the costume of manual laborers) and of artistic caprice. James Dean has invented nothing; he has canonized and codified an ensemble of sumptuary laws that allows an age class to assert itself, and this age class will assert itself even further in imitation of its hero.

James Dean, in his double life, both on and off the screen, is a pure hero of adolescence. He expresses his needs and his revolt in a single impulse that the French and English titles of one of his films express: *La fureur de vivre (A Rage to Live)* and *Rebel without a Cause* are two aspects of the same virulent demand, in which a rebellious fury confronts a life without a cause.

Because he is a hero of adolescence, James Dean expresses with a clarity rare in American films, in *East of Eden* and *Rebel without a Cause*, the rebellion against the family. The American film tends to mask parent-child conflicts, either in the familial idyll (the Hardy family) or else by altogether suppressing the parents' existence and transferring the father's image onto an insensible, cruel, or ridiculous old man (half-senile judge or employer). *East of Eden* presents

the characters of an uncomprehending father and a fallen mother; *Rebel without a Cause* presents the characters of an uncomprehending mother and a fallen father. In both these films appear the theme of the adolescent's combat against the father (whether the latter is tyrannical or pitiful) and the theme of his inability to relate meaningfully to his mother. In *Giant*, the framework of the conflict explodes: it is against a family exterior to himself and, by extension, against all social norms that James Dean will do battle with such ferocious hatred.[2]

But in all three films appears the common theme of the woman-sister who must be snatched from someone else's possession. In other words, the problem of sexual love is still enclosed within a sororal-maternal love, has not yet broken out of this shell to launch itself in a universe of pinups external to family and age class alike. Upon these imaginary movie loves is superimposed the love, itself also mythical perhaps, that Dean is supposed to have felt for Pier Angeli,

with her ingenuous, sister-madonna face. Beyond this impossible love begins the universe of sexual "adventures."

In another sense James Dean expresses in his life and films the needs of adolescent individuality, which, asserting itself, refused to accept the norms of the soul-killing and specialized life that lie ahead. The demand for a total life, the quest for the absolute, is every human individual's demand when he tears himself from the nest of childhood and the chains of the family only to see before him the new chains and mutilations of social life. It is then that the most contradictory requirements come to a ferment. Truffaut expresses it perfectly:

> In James Dean, today's youth discovers itself. Less for
> the reasons usually advanced: violence, sadism, hysteria,
> pessimism, cruelty, and filth, than for others infinitely
> more simple and commonplace: modesty of feeling,
> continual fantasy life, moral purity without relation to
> everyday morality but all the more rigorous; eternal

adolescent love of tests and trials, intoxication, pride, and regret at feeling oneself "outside" society, refusal and desire to become integrated and, finally, acceptance—or refusal—of the world as it is.[3]

The essential contradiction is the one that links the most intense aspiration to a total life with the greatest possibility of death. This contradiction is the problem of virile initiation, which is resolved in primitive societies by terrible institutionalized tests of endurance. In our society it is effected institutionally only by war (and vestigially by military service); lacking war or collective subversions (revolutions, underground resistance), this initiation must be sought in individual risk.

Finally the adult of our middle-class bureaucratized society is the man who agrees to live only a little in order not to die a great deal. But the secret of adolescence is that living *means* risking death, that the rage to live *means* the

impossibility of living. James Dean has lived this contradiction and authenticated it by his death.

These themes of adolescence appear with great clarity at a period when adolescence is particularly reduced to its own resources, when society allows it no outlets by which it can engage or even recognize its cause. A James Dean has not been able to become an exemplary figure in these years of the half century by chance. To the intense participations of the war and (in France) of the Resistance, to the immense hopes of 1944–46, have succeeded not only individualist withdrawals but a generalized nihilism that is a radical interrogation of all official ideologies and values. The ideological lie in which contemporary societies live, pretending to be harmonious, happy, and uplifting, provokes in return this "nihilism" or this "romanticism" in which adolescence both escapes and discovers the reality of life.

It is at this point in the Western middle-class world that adventures, risk, and death participate in the gunning of a motorcycle or a racing car: already the motorcyclists of *Orpheus* left death's fatal wake behind them, already László Benedek's *The Wild One* traced bitterly and tenderly the image of the adolescent motorcyclist. Marlon Brando, roaring archangel, like an imaginary John the Baptist heralded the real James Dean because he himself was the imaginary expression of thousands of real adolescents whose only expression of their rage to live as rebels without a cause was the motorcycle gang. Motorized *speed* is not only one of the modern signs of the quest for the absolute but corresponds to the need for risk and self-affirmation in everyday life. Anyone behind a wheel feels like a god in the most biblical sense of the term, self-intoxicated, ready to strike other drivers with thunderbolts, terrorize mortals (pedestrians), and hand down the law in the form of insults to all who do not recognize his *absolute priority*.

The automobile is escape at last: Rimbaud's sandals of the wind are replaced by James Dean's big racing Porsche. And the supreme escape is death, just as the absolute is death, just as the supreme individuality is death. James Dean drives into the night toward the death from which the contract to make *Giant* could protect him only temporarily.

Death fulfills the destiny of every mythological hero by fulfilling his double nature: human and divine. It fulfills his profound humanity, which is to struggle heroically against the world, to confront heroically a death that ultimately overwhelms him. At the same time, death fulfills the superhuman nature of the hero: it divinizes him by opening wide the gates of immortality. Only after his sacrifice, in which he expiates his human condition, does Jesus become a god.

Thus amplified in the character of James Dean are the phenomena of divinization that characterize but generally remain atrophied in the movie stars. First of all, that spontaneous, naive phenomenon: the refusal to believe in the

hero's death. The death of Napoleon, Hitler, of every superman (good or evil) has been doubted and disbelieved because the faithful were never able to believe these heroes
were entirely mortal. The death of James Dean has been
similarly doubted. There is a legend that he miraculously
survived his accident, that it was a hitchhiker who was
killed, that James Dean was disfigured, unrecognizable, perhaps unconscious; that he has been shut up somewhere in an
insane asylum or a hospital. Every week, two thousand letters are mailed to a living James Dean. Living where? In a
no-man's-land between life and death that the modern mind
chooses to situate in insane asylums and sanitariums but
that cannot be localized. Here James Dean offers himself to
the spiritualist conception of death: James Dean is among
us, invisible and present. Spiritualism revives the primitive
notion according to which the dead, who are corporeal specters endowed with invisibility and ubiquity, live among the
living. This is why one young girl cried out, "Come back,
Jimmy, I love you! We're waiting for you!" during a showing
of *Giant*. It is the *living* (spiritualist) presence of James Dean
that his fanatics will henceforth look for in his films. This is
why spiritualist seances held to communicate with James
Dean have multiplied. This is why the little dime-store
salesgirl, Joan Collins, took from the dictation of the dead
James Dean the extraordinary spiritualist confession in
which he declares, "I am not dead. Those who believe I am
not dead are right," and in which he asserts he has rejoined
his mother. This is why *James Dean Returns* by Joan Collins
has sold more than five hundred thousand copies.

Thus a cult has been organized, like all cults, in order to
reestablish contact between mortals and the immortal dead.
James Dean's tomb is constantly covered with flowers, and
three thousand people made a pilgrimage there on the first
anniversary of his death. His death mask will be placed be-
side those of Beethoven, Thackeray, and Keats at Princeton
University. His bust in plaster is on sale for thirty dollars.

The fatal car has become a sacred object. For a quarter you can look at the big racing Porsche, for an additional quarter you can sit behind the wheel. This ruined car, which symbolizes the Passion of James Dean, his rage to live and his rage to die, has been dismembered: bolts and screws, bits of twisted metal, regarded as sacred relics, can be bought at prices starting at twenty dollars, according to size, and carried about like amulets to imbue the wearer with the hero's mystic substance.

In death, by means of death, James Dean has recovered the forgotten prestige of the stars of the great epoch who, nearer gods than mortals, aroused hysterical adoration. But from another point of view his death authenticates a life that firmly fixes him among the modern stars, within the reach of mortals. The modern stars are models and examples, whereas the earlier ones were the ideals of a dream. James Dean is a real hero, but one who undergoes a divinization analogous to that of the great stars of the silent films.

And the immortality of James Dean is also his collective survival in a thousand mimetisms. James Dean is indeed a perfect star: god, hero, model. But this perfection, if it has been able to fulfill itself only by means of the star system, derives from the life and death of the real James Dean and from the exigence that is his own as well as that of a generation that sees itself in him, reflected and transfigured in twin mirrors: screen and death.

Une vedette en or!
GRACE
KELLY

Star Merchandise

The star is a goddess. The public makes her one. But the star system prepares her, trains her, molds her, moves her, manufactures her. The star corresponds to an affective or mythic need that the star system does not create, but without the star system this need would not find its forms, its supports, its excitants.

The star system is a specific institution of capitalism on a major scale. Before the period of Stalinist hero worship, the Soviet cinema attempted to eliminate not only the star but even the leading player. Now great character actors common to stage and screen generally play the leading parts. Their prestige of course extends beyond the screen, but it has hitherto been channeled and "ennobled" by politics. The genius of Soviet leading actors, like that of any Stakhanovite record breaker, runner, prima ballerina, or eminent writer, is used to prove the excellence of the Soviet system and attests to a political merit eventually worthy of consecration by service to the Supreme Soviet. A certain kind of star might eventually appear in the USSR to satisfy imaginative needs that are at present meagerly fulfilled. But any cinema in the contemporary world that situates itself outside of, on the margins of, or in competition with capitalism, even at an underdeveloped capitalist level, does not have stars in the sense of the term as we understand it in the West. The tendency of the "cinema of truth" in its "documentary" or "neorealist" developments, from Flaherty's *Nanook of the North* to Renoir's *Toni* and Visconti's *La terra trema*, radically eliminates the star and, eventually, even the professional actor. It is precisely the fundamental tendency of the cinema that is independent of trusts and combines or is in rebellion against them.

At a lower level of capitalist production, minor film productions are materially forced to do without the luxury of a star (B pictures in the United States, films costing less than fifty million francs in France). Furthermore, the cinema was unaware of the star at its first industrial and commercial stage. The star was born in 1910 out of the fierce competition of the first film companies in the United States. The star developed simultaneously with the concentration of capital at the heart of the film industry, these two developments mutually accelerating each other. The great stars have progressively become the appanage and property of the major studios, as they have become the appanage and center of gravity of the major films.

The star system has formed itself progressively: it is not so much a consequence as a specific element of these developments. Its internal characteristics are indeed those of industrial mercantile and financial capitalism on a major scale. The star system is first of all *production*. The word was used spontaneously by Carl Laemmle, the inventor of the stars: "The production of the stars is a prime necessity in the film industry." We have indicated in a preceding chapter how a veritable production line snatches up the pretty girls unearthed by the talent scout, rationalizes, standardizes, sifts, eliminates defective parts, sorts, assembles, molds, polishes, beautifies, and, in a word, produces. The manufactured product undergoes the last tests, is sneak previewed, and launched. If it triumphs on the market, it still remains under the control of the manufacturer: the star's private life is prefabricated, rationally organized.

Meanwhile, the manufactured product has become merchandise. The star has her price, of course, and this price regularly follows the fluctuations of supply and demand, the latter regularly estimated by the box office and the fan mail department. Furthermore, as Bachlin points out, "a star's way of life is in itself merchandise."[1] The private-public life of the stars is always endowed with a commercial—that is, advertising—effectiveness. Let us add that the star is not only a subject but an object of advertising. She sponsors perfumes, soaps, cigarettes, and so on, and thereby multiplies her commercial utility.

The star is a total item of merchandise: there is not an inch of her body, not a shred of her soul, not a memory of her life that cannot be thrown on the market. This total merchandise has other virtues: she is the typical merchandise of capitalism on a major scale. The enormous investments, the system's industrial techniques of rationalization and standardization, effectively convert the star into merchandise destined for mass consumption. The star has all the virtues of a standard product adapted to the world market, like chewing gum, refrigerators, soap, razor blades, and so on. Mass distribution is assured by the greatest diffusers

in the modern world: the press, radio, and, of course, the movies.

Furthermore, star merchandise neither wears out nor diminishes upon consumption. The multiplication of a star's images, far from impairing, augments her worth and makes her more desirable. In other words, the star remains original, rare, and unique even when she is widely distributed and used. The highly precious matrix of her own images, she is a kind of frozen capital and at the same time an asset in the commercial sense of the term, like the mines of Rio Tinto or the Parentis oil fields. Thus Wall Street banks have a special office in which are assessed from day to day Betty Grable's legs, Jayne Mansfield's bust, Bing Crosby's voice,

Fred Astaire's feet. The star is simultaneously standard merchandise, luxury item, and a source of capital gains. She is capital merchandise. The star is like *gold:* a material so precious that it is identified with the very notion of capital, with the very notion of luxury (jewelry), and confers a value on fiduciary money. Gold holdings in the vaults of banks have guaranteed for centuries, as economists say, but above all mystically endowed, paper money. Similarly, Hollywood's star holdings make each can of film redeemable. Gold and star are two mythical powers that dizzily attract and arrest every human ambition.

Microcosm of capitalism, the star is something like jewels, spices, rare objects, precious metals, the search for which brought the Middle Ages out of its economic paralysis. She is also like those manufactured products of which industrial capitalism assures a mass multiplication. After the raw materials and the goods of material consumption are obtained, industrial techniques have to take over the dreams of the human heart: press, radio, and cinema have revealed the prodigious marketability of dreams, a raw material as free and plastic as the wind, which needs only to be formulated and standardized in order to correspond to the fundamental archetypes of the imagination.

The standard product was one day to encounter the archetype; the gods were one day to be manufactured; the myths were to become merchandise; and the human mind was to enter the circuit of industrial production, not only as engineer, but as consumer and consumer goods as well. The bread of dreams, it will be said, but with this difference: that while the selling price of bread can rise only slightly above production cost, all products endowed with magic or mystical value are sold at prices far in excess of their production costs—medicines, makeup, dentifrices, ornaments, fetishes, objets d'art, and stars too.

The star is as rare as gold and as common as bread. Born in 1910 from the competition for control of the film market, she has understandably created the development of the capitalist industry of the cinema as much as this industry has created her. From their common rise was conceived and institutionalized the star system, a machine for producing, sustaining, and exalting the stars, upon which are focused and flower into divinization of the magical virtualities the screen image. The star is a specific product of capitalist civilization; at the same time, she satisfies profound anthropological needs that are expressed at the level of myth and religion. The admirable coincidence of myth and capital, of goddess and merchandise, is neither fortuitous nor contradictory. Star-goddess and star merchandise are two faces of the same reality: the needs of man at the stage of twentieth-century capitalist civilization.

The Star and the Actor

G oddess-object, the star is of course something more than an actress who makes movies. But the star is *also* an actress who makes movies. The ethnography, psychology, sociology, and economy of the star system must be completed or illuminated by a "filmology." It is to the degree that the movie actor is not a stage actor that the star is possible.

The stage actor's performance is determined by certain practical necessities. The distance separating stage from spectator requires an exaggeration of voice and gestures; the actor, as Dullin says, must magnify emotion. Conversely, whereas the "stage actor generally plays in a major key, the movie actor generally plays in the minor."[1] As René Simon puts it, "He must subtract instead of multiply."

Nevertheless, the early films took their original bearings in relation to the theater and annexed all the procedures of stage expression *(The Assassination of the Duke de Guise).* They even multiplied tenfold the "theatricality" of the actor, who, denied words, expressed himself in the language of mime. But after the years 1915–20 bodies progressively abandoned these gesticulations, faces became immobilized (Sessue Hayàkawa, Adolph Menjou, Red La Roque, Eve Francis, Lillian

Gish, Norma Talmadge). *This detheatricalization of the actor's performance in spite of the absence of sound goes hand in hand with the development of the cinema's techniques. It is the consequence of this development.*

In effect the camera's mobility, either within the same shot or from close-up to long shot, and the cutting of montages shot from different angles and distances will constitute, as Pudovkin says, "the most vital and expressive equivalent of the acting technique which obliges a stage actor . . . to theatricalize the image exterior to his own personality."[2] In other words, for the expressive art of the actor the film substitutes an expressive art of camera and cutting.

The close-up, an American technique, destroys the distance that in the theater separates actor from spectator and renders superfluous the ostentation of gesture and mime. "A stage actor is a little head in a huge hall, a movie actor a huge head in a little hall" (Malraux). The expressive capacities of this "huge head" supplant those of all gesture and render useless even the conventional sign language of the face: henceforth the merest trembling of the lips and fluttering of the lashes are visible, therefore legible, therefore eloquent. The actor has no need to exaggerate his expressions. The close-up exaggerates them for him.

The development of the talkies struck a final blow at the mime technique that the silent film could still eventually require of its interpreters. Of course the first movie voices resuscitated oral and aural theatricality. Henri Garat and Albert Préjean seemed to be talking into the wings. But increasingly sensitive microphones have permitted the use of a conversational tone, a mezza voce, a murmur, a whisper. The voice has ceased to be ritual, modulated, theatrical. Edwige Feuillère points out that "the defect most generally observed in film actors on the stage is a great monotony of delivery."[3] Here too the cinema destroys emphasis—that is, part of the actor's technique.

The cinema does not merely detheatricalize the actor's

performance. It tends to atrophy it. The stage actor, although his performance has been determined in advance during rehearsals, is more or less left to himself on the stage. The movie actor is constantly directed in the dispersed and fragmentary shots that are being filmed. He follows the cameraman's chalk marks, pitches his voice according to the sound engineer's instructions, obeys the director's sign language. This discipline makes all performances automatic, and furthermore the director eventually relies on Pavlovian reflexes: The star can't cry? He slaps her. A little well-placed tickling can make her burst out laughing as spontaneously as a camera could desire. Thus she can *automatically* express grief or joy.

To meet these particular conditions of an automatic, pulverized performance, the movies can demand superior actors, actors capable of expressing their roles even without the support of an immediate public and deprived of the accumulated energy that continuity of conception and unity of role provide on the stage. On the other hand, the cinema can simply content itself with automata, since spectator participation is particularly active in the cinema.

All affective participation is a complex of projections and identifications. In life, either spontaneously or at the suggestion of tokens or signs, everyone transfers to someone else certain feelings and ideas naively attributed to that person. These phenomena of projection-identification are excited by every spectacle: an action involves our psychic participation more generally when we are purely spectators, that is, physically passive. We live the spectacle in an almost mystical fashion, mentally integrating ourselves with the characters and the action (projection) and mentally integrating them with ourselves (identification).

Spectacle of spectacles, the movies can excite projections to a point where they bestow expression on what is inexpressive, accord a soul to what is inanimate, give life to what is inert. Kuleshov's experiment, which played such a great

role in the growth of the cinema's self-awareness, demonstrates that the situation of objects and characters within an isolated shot suffices to determine, in the spectator's eyes, an expression on the inexpressive face of the actor. Kuleshov superimposed the same shot of the actor Mosjoukine on shots of a bowl of soup, a dead woman, a laughing baby, and spectators marveled at the actor's admirable expressions of appetite, grief, paternal joy.

In other words, the given situation and the elements of this situation (objects, decor) can play a greater role than the actor and *express for him*. Whereas in the theater the actor illuminates the situation, in the cinema it is the situation that illuminates the actor. The decor becomes a part of the character's physiognomy, whereas in the theater the decor is limited to localizing and suggesting it.

If the stage actor's performance essentially determines projection-identification, the movie actor's performance can be determined by it, can henceforth be atrophied or nonexistent: the character will not cease to live and to express. These phenomena of projection-identification, already known and employed in certain theatrical traditions (marionette theaters, the Japanese theater), are here amplified in a specific manner.

It is first of all the *doubled* nature of the cinematic image, its character as a "mirror" or a "reflection" of reality, that determines its particular spell. The cinematic image itself creates the affective participation or imaginary identification-participation; the very situation of the spectator—aesthetic relaxation, darkness, parahypnotic state—promotes this process.

At the heart of this cinematic situation (doubled image, spectator's parahypnotic relaxation), the film develops an imaginary action according to a real dynamic hitherto unknown. Murders, battles, wild rides, every violence of love and death break loose on the screen, while on the stage only Theramène's tirade about actions can trick us into believing in them. The film's dynamic stimulates affective participation.

To this dynamic of action is added an internal dynamic,

the montage. The montage is a system of fragmentary and discontinuous images that are linked with one another according to a certain rhythm, thereby assuming a total and continuous significance *precisely because the montage is completely based on the spectator's projection-identification mechanisms.* It implies them, solicits them, at the same time it accelerates and amplifies them. Thus every phenomenon of projection-identification already apparent within a single shot (as in the Kuleshov experiment) is multiplied tenfold in the systematic succession of shots (montage). Not only the situation but the succession of situations, the action, the cinematic *system* illuminate the actor, *give life* to the actor, *act for* the actor. In the alternation of parallel scenes at the dynamic peak of the action (the villain persecuting the captive heroine, the hero galloping toward them) the actor's performance has no importance whatsoever. The cutting and montage can entirely substitute for what, in the theater, depended on the actor's ability to "project beyond the footlights." Which is why film technicians say that good cutting can save a bad actor.

Cutting and montage multiply the results of the Kuleshov effect. The spectator's projection-identification, spurred by the rhythm of the film (to which are added the music, the lighting effects, the movements and positions of the camera), gives life and *presence* not only to the inexpressive countenance of the actor but even to objects without faces. As we have elsewhere shown, projection becomes anthropomorphism: the revolver, the handkerchief, the tree, the car not only *express* feelings, but assume life and presence. They speak to us, they act. Reciprocally the inexpressive countenances are charged with a message that transcends them: they are filled with a cosmic presence, they become landscapes. To the anthropomorphism of things corresponds the cosmomorphism of faces. Thus the actor has no need to express everything or, in extreme cases, to express anything; objects, action, the film itself will do this acting for him.

The cinema can confine itself entirely to automata, not only to the degree that the requirements of the shooting schedule bind the actor to an automatic technique; not only to the degree that the effects of projection-identification created by the screen image, the dynamic contents of the film, and the cutting and montage function actively and automatically in place of the actor; but also to the degree that specific techniques, techniques exterior to the actor, artificially *prefabricate* feelings that hitherto had been inspired only by an individual actor's performance.

Aside from such subterfuges as glycerine tears, a system of emotive and significant techniques (camera position, duration of image, filters) works on the actor as if he were raw material. Angle shots are potentially charged with affective significance: an upward shot ennobles a character, confers greatness, authority, power, whereas a shot from above foreshortens and humiliates. Camera speed and duration of image mechanically determine emotions that the spectator believes are expressed by the face itself. A sudden close-up can produce a surprised, anxious, or terrified countenance; and the same inexpressive face expresses humor, indifference, or grief according to the reduced, medium, or extended duration of the image on the screen. To camera techniques we must add those of lighting. "A good part of the feelings which the actor must express are already expressed for him in the arrangement of the lighting."[4] A face in shadow is threatening; brilliantly lit, it is gay; lit from below, it is bestial; from above, radiant with spirituality.

Completing the artifices of photography, the artifices of makeup can transform the physiognomy according to the expression required by each shot. Thus, as Sadoul remarks of the touching face of Michèle Morgan as the drowned girl in *La symphonie pastorale*, "Much more than the work of the artist herself, this image was the product of the collective labor of the makeup man and the hairdresser who gave the face its overwhelming quality, of the cameraman who

provided its tragic lighting, of the cutting-room which determined the duration the image required, and finally and
especially of the director."[5]

All of these techniques (camera movements, choice and
duration of shots, lighting, music) coat the face and the gestures with the expressive intensity they may have lacked or
multiply the impression they may eventually produce. They
can be more important to the actor's expression than his
own expression and, of course, more important than his lack
of it.

Thus it is the very film system that tends to disintegrate
the actor. The actor can even be physically divided, leaving
on the screen only a grasping hand, a foot advancing toward
another foot, a back turned—and this hand, this foot, this
back take the place of words, expressions of the face, pos-
ture, even movements of the body. Sometimes the body is
completely eliminated and only the voice substituted. The
actor's voice, while the camera focuses on something else—
an event, a character, an object—not only suggests his presence but can be more affecting than that presence itself.
Conversely, the cinema can completely eliminate the actor's
voice, either by making objects or situations speak in his
place or by replacing it with someone else's voice that will
be more effective. Stand-ins, doubles, and dubbing bear witness to the actor's borderline utility: someone else, someone quite anonymous, can replace the actor or his voice
without inconveniencing the spectator or even making him
conscious of what has happened. The constant use of doubles and of dubbing is thus an exemplary test of the molec-
ular decomposition of an individuality hitherto sovereign:
that of the actor.

Within limits, the spectator continues to *see* the invisible
actor and to read on his invisible countenance the feelings
that move him. Anthropo-cosmomorphism makes *things* act
for him. They even replace the actor advantageously; hence
Alexandre Arnoux's definition: "A great movie actor . . . is a

man who is not outplayed by his dog, his horse, or his gun," Hence also Leslie Howard's observation: "Actors can be eliminated and replaced by anything at all."

Thus, to sum up, the actor's performance is only one means of cinematic expression that can always be canceled out; on the other hand, the direction of the actors can constitute the essential art of certain films.[6]

To be an actor requires neither training nor skill. Which is why there is no professional instruction for movie actors in many countries. And why movie actors, and not the least effective ones, beginning with the stars, come, quite simply, off the street. And why children do not even need to know—to live—their roles ("I didn't know I had been so unhappy," exclaimed little Paulette Elambert after seeing *La maternelle*). And why animals—Rin Tin Tin, Cheetah—interpret with perfect naturalness the most anthropomorphic roles, that is, the most artificial roles.

On the set, actors are a little like children or animals: unspecified and unspecialized raw material under the direction of real *technicians* who are the engineers, mechanics, cameramen, directors. They can even be reduced to the condition of objects. "We stars are furniture, furniture of more or less value, more or less authentic furniture, but furniture all the same for the director to arrange on the set" (Jean Chevrier); "Robots wound up and set going by director's hands" (A. Luguet). Pierre Renoir, Jouvet, Marie Bell, Edwige Feuillère all frequently declared that the actor is worth only what the director can make of him. Moussinac writes: "The cinematic artist is theoretically only photographic material, intelligent or stupid according to the decisions of the director in relation to the purpose of his work. . . . the quality of a particular expression is subordinated to the quality of expression of the whole."[7] Sadoul: "The director sometimes uses the actor like a musical instrument, asking only that he emit . . . a note on pitch which will later comprise an element of the great symphony."[8] Delluc does not include the actor among the four essential elements of cinematic expression, which for him are decor, lighting, cadence, and mask. According to Delluc, the actor's face (mask) is treated as decor. The actor thus tends to become an automaton, a mask, a marionette, or, as Mussorgsky called him, "a talking statue." As a matter of fact, the Trnka marionettes and Walt Disney's Mickey Mouse and Donald Duck are as *lifelike* as many actors, and perhaps more so.

Ultimately we arrive at the notion, on the one hand, of the actor who has been volatilized, replaced by anyone at all: the man in the street, the ignorant child—or by anything at all: the marionette, the animated cartoon—and, on the other, of the actor who is not an actor at all, that is, totally inexpressive.

But the miracle is that the stupid actor is effective and even profound *in the movies*, that the film makes a foolish actor real and touching. This miracle derives from the spectator's *projection*, which, if it gives life to the inanimate objects of the screen, gives life *a fortiori* to the marionettes that are actors. *The cinema exalts the role at the same time that it destroys the actor.*

First of all, the presences on the screen radiate a kind of diffused prestige, the glamour of the double. Corporeal and yet elusive specters, "the shadow personalities the film presents seem to the spectator more real, more human, more intensely themselves than actors of flesh and blood behind the footlights."[9] These shadow personalities are further magnified by the close-up, by lighting, makeup, music, and so on—that is, by precisely those techniques that destroy the actor's performance. These techniques, which unite their effectiveness in the cutting room, flood the human countenance with an infinite wealth of participations.

The physical absence of the actor contributes to this exaltation of the role. Of course the stage actor submits to the *adhesion* of the role he is interpreting, but for the audience he only associates himself with that role after the applause that greets his arrival on the stage and dissociates himself from it for his curtain calls. The stage actor shows through his character at each blunder, at each act of valor.

The movie actor must adhere so closely to his role that he is chosen as a function of his type, that is, of the immediate, natural signification and expression of his face and body. As Pudovkin puts it, "The diversity of roles which the movie actor can play depends either on the diversity of types he can interpret while preserving the same exterior appearance (von Stroheim), or on the development of the same type through a diversity of circumstances."[10] The facial type, the dominant and characteristic expression of the features, assumes such an importance that the director goes into the street to look for new faces and makes use of what he finds. Therefore it is less important to have features that can act than to have features in the first place—to have a mask. The physical *type* tends to equal or surpass in significance the traditional imitative skill of the character actor. Hence there are fewer and fewer character actors on the screen today. Here too there is a promotion of the character, the role, and a simultaneous devaluation of the actor's *performance*.

The actor's performance is nevertheless not entirely deprived of meaning and interest in the movies, but is henceforth based on a particular dialectic. "Be natural," the actors are told. Being natural becomes, somehow, the only technique in which they are actually given instruction. Hollywood starlets learn how to talk, walk, run, sit, descend stairs. J. Arthur Rank's Company of Youth (founded in 1946) gives lessons in dancing, walking, fencing—that is, lessons in grace, animal suppleness, life itself. "The actor is obliged to be as natural as a tree."[11] But at the same time this movie naturalness becomes a stylization, a nonrealism, since unlike a tree the characteristic of man is to lack naturalness in his clumsiness, blunders, stammers, nonsense. Hence a new dialectic of the natural and artificial, which leads the actor to create certain *tics*—twitching his coat, running his hands through his hair, not to mention the key sign of the "natural": lighting a cigarette. And an actor is considered great in this "natural" genre precisely when he transcends both tics *and* stereotyped naturalness, gracefully recovering blunder and stammer, and seeming to invent, with each gesture, his own naturalness.

At the same time that it encourages "naturalness," the cinema encourages a *ritual* based on the hieratic quality of the mask and the automatism of the doll, a ritual congruent in a sense with the ritual of the Greek and Japanese theaters and of the marionette theater as well. Movie acting begins with the frozen face of Sessue Hayakawa (*The Cheat*, Cecil B. DeMille, 1915) and has subsequently oriented itself, in the close-up, toward "that art which I regard as the basis of our own, the art of precise masks."[12]

At the two poles of the movie actor's performance are the mask and "naturalness." They can alternate according to the requirements of the shot or the qualities of the actor, or they can unite in what is called "the quiet face." "The quiet face" makes every effort to reconcile the permanent expression of the mask with the thousand tiny lifelike expressions that constitute "naturalness." It is acquired in front of the cameras by an interiorization of the performance. Murnau used to tell his actors, "Don't act. Think!"[13] In 1915 Jacques de Baroncelli was saying, "You must not step into your character's shoes, but into his thoughts." And Charles Dullin: "In the cinema the actor must think and let his thoughts work upon his face. The objective nature of the medium will do the rest. . . . A theatrical performance requires magnification, a cinema performance requires an inner life."[14] The requirement of an inner life here completes Kuleshov's theory of "living models."

"Think!" This cinematic cogito is clear. The movie actor's "I think" is an "I am." Being is more important than manifesting. "Acting is not living, it is being" (Jean Epstein).

The actor's "I am" assumes its importance as "*an act of faith in his double*."

The screen performance becomes a performance of souls: the close-ups of faces are "veritable cross-sections of the soul."[15] The lucidity in Michèle Morgan's eyes is like a mine shaft into the soul. As Dullin remarks in the article quoted above, "The cinema asks for a soul behind the face." Eve Francis: "Act with your soul in the depths of your eyes."[16] The repression of gestures and body movements tends to draw all attention toward "the soul of the face." The movie actor's performance is not necessarily abolished, but tends to metamorphose itself into the art of subjective presence within the framework established by the living model (the mask or expressive type).

Hence the possibilities unknown or barely suspected in the theater that the cinema has been able to exploit. First of all, the "quiet face"—"concentrated," "natural," "realistic," "psychological"—which can express itself in movements at the extreme limit of perceptibility. On the other hand, the actor tends to interpret characters that are really his own. According to Frank Capra, Gary Cooper played himself as Mr. Deeds. The specialization of an actor as a function of his "type" in the movies assumes a scope unknown in the theater. "Naturalness" has everything to gain by it, of course: "Every actor reaches his peak when he is told to express himself in a character that resembles him like a brother" (Capra).

The director can pursue the identity of actor and role, beyond professionals, among unknowns whose physical, sociological types correspond to the characters required by the film. First the Soviet (Eisenstein, Pudovkin) then the Italian directors (Rossellini, de Sica) have used these men in the street. "One must find in a crowd the faces, the expressions, the heads one wants to have."[17] "You must not be afraid of people who are not professional actors. You must remember that each man can play himself perfectly on the screen at least once."[18] For "an actual old man has a sixty-year head start in preparing his role."[19]

Of course, the "naturalness" of nonprofessionals has its limits. "Since the studio seems non-natural to them, they make themselves non-natural."[20] But this restriction can be avoided by psychodramatic and sociodramatic devices on the part of the director. Actually it is the professional experience of "typed" actors and the development of the stars that have restricted the utilization of more bicycle thieves.

In direct proportion to their denial of the traditional actor, the movies have created the star. The star derives from the "natural" actor, the "typed" actor, and not from the professional nonactor. Like the nonactor or the specialized actor, the star is an expressive type. What distinguishes her are the superior and ideal qualities that make her an *archetype*. Like the specialized actor and the nonactor—and unlike the character actor and the theater actor—the star plays her own character, that is, the ideal character that her face, her smile, her eyes, her lovely body naturally express (Asta Nielsen, Mary Pickford, Lillian Gish, Valentino). "The generations of the theater went to see Booth in *Othello*, Mansfield in *Cyrano* . . . we go to see Garbo in Garbo."[21]

The star permanently plays her own character (even in life, as we have seen), with a few piquant exceptions (Garbo laughs!). The cinema even goes so far as to appropriate champions (Marcel Cerdan, Sonja Henie) and orchestra conductors (Leopold Stokowski) to interpret their own roles, sometimes under their own identities.

We here rejoin the dialectic from which a star is born, proceeding from the real character to the screen character and reciprocally. Let us only remember that if the star acts out her myth (her screen character) in life, this myth is already inscribed in her type—her face and her body. For these faces, these bodies, these voices that the cinema selects are already, in life, bearers of a kind of sacred mystery.

These faces are the masks that immediately express strength or tenderness, innocence or experience, virility or kindness, and more generally a superhuman quality, a divine harmony, that we call *beauty*.

Our admiration and our love charge these beautiful faces with radiant souls. Physical beauty always seems to us an interior richness, a cosmic depth. It is the transparent envelope of the beautiful soul. The beauty of these multiple faces is the sacred mask that, of itself and in our behalf, expresses virtue, truth, justice, love. Beauty is a language. *Whereas the expression of the ravaged, eroded, hairy faces of Eisenstein's close-ups constitutes their beauty, it is the beauty of the radiant faces of the stars, proffered like a brimming cup, lips half open, that constitutes their expression.*

Unlike the theater, in films the actor's beauty can reveal itself as both the necessary and the sufficient determinant. *Beauty is the actress in the movies.* The star can be entirely inexpressive: her performance, as Emil Ludwig once said, can be reduced to "a single intonation, a single facial *tic*, a single gesture that she repeats in every role in which she appears." Leo Rosten describes a star who has only two expressions: joy and indigestion. But this star's beauty can be as moving, as magical, as effective as the sacred masks of China, India, and Greece. As eloquent as the beauty of statues.

Here where the maximum destruction of the actor and the maximum exaltation of the role are in operation, the star needs to do nothing beyond cultivate her beauty, acquire a superior grace, and sustain her semimythic personality. Anyone at all can be a star, Shirley Temple or Ava Gardner, big doll or tiny. An infinite power of projection will focus itself on this doll to accord it the supreme, divine expression. *Inexpressiveness is the supreme expression of beauty. The techniques of the cinema complete the transformation of the doll into an idol.*

The stars, Malraux has said, are not actresses who make movies. They are actresses, but some of them cannot attain even the minimum degree of expression. Yet it is the same public that admires the intelligent performances of Emil Jannings, Michel Simon, Charles Laughton, the great ugly men of the movies, that also admires the infinite void of the beautiful faces onto which it projects its own soul. There is no contradiction. Beauty is an effective equivalent of all the other virtues—when it is not, indeed, the supreme virtue!

Of course it is not indispensable that the star have no talent. Knowing how to act doesn't spoil anything. Some great actresses are also stars, like Katharine Hepburn, Bette Davis, Anna Magnani. In France, according to Gentilhomme, thirteen out of every twenty stars are stage actresses as well.

We have also indicated the further exception of the comic star. His performance remains the most faithful to the traditions of the circus, music hall, and theater: it preserves the exaggeration of gesture, the skill of mimicry, and ultimately the sense of the word-as-joke. Comedy is an art, a talent, a technique. It is not a matter of chance that a number of great dramatic actors have first of all been great clowns, like Chaplin or Raimu. The comic order, a veritable negative of the dramatic or the tragic, shows us again that the scale of profane and sacrilegious emotions—laughter, in a word—can be mechanized the least, is the most *intelligent*. With the exception of the comic, as well as of eventual expressive talent on the part of the stars, it is nonetheless true that the star system has developed only because film techniques have transformed and disintegrated the ancient conception of the actor.

The nonactor and the star are the end products of the same need, a need not for an actor but for a type, for a living model, a presence. The minimum degree of expressive cinematic performance, which permits the annihilation of the actor, occasionally produces a certain extreme type of star based on beauty: the star who is automaton and mask, object and divinity. The star is a star because it has been possible to transform actors into objects that are manipulated by

film technicians, and because it has been possible to endow a face-mask, one that is often already charged with all the adorable glamour of beauty, with all the subjective riches as well. The star is a star because the technical system of the film develops and excites a projection-identification culminating in divinization precisely when focusing on what man knows to be the most affecting thing in the world: a beautiful human face.

The Star and Us

After having examined the psychological, sociological, and economic conditions of the star system, we have just considered its specifically cinematic conditions. The star-object (merchandise) and the star-goddess (myth) are possible because the techniques of the movies excite and exalt a system of participations that affect the actor in both performance and personality.

Of course the star was—and is—only one of the possibilities of the movies. She was not, as we have pointed out, a necessary condition of the basic nature of cinematic expression. But the latter has made her possible. Another cinema, one founded on "nonactors," might have taken hold equally well. But the capitalist economy and the mythology of the modern world, and essentially the mythology of love, have determined this hypertrophy, this hydrocephalism, this sacred monstrosity: the star.

Film heroes and their exploits, the sound and the fury that surround them, dissolve into the spectator's mind. But this very evaporation liberates certain pacifying effluvia. Thus the star, heroine of the movies, participates in the role of aesthetic purification that is the function of every spectacle.

But the star is a star precisely to the degree that the role she plays overflows the boundaries of aesthetic considerations. As the investigations of H. Blumer and J. P. Mayer indicate, the star chooses her place in the mind of her admirers. She continues to live on the screen the dreams of sleep and the dreams of waking. She maintains and molds these dreams, that is, imaginary identification. As one young English girl puts it, "I dream of Rita Hayworth and I play all her roles in my dreams."

The star, then, becomes the provender of dreams: dreams, unlike Aristotle's ideal tragedy, do not really purge us of our fantasies but betray their obsessive presence: thus the stars provoke only a partial catharsis and foster fantasies that for all their yearning cannot release themselves in actions. The star's role becomes *psychotic:* she polarizes and fixes obsessions. Yet if these dreams cannot transform themselves into total acts, they nevertheless crop out on the surface of our concrete lives, mold our behavior at its most plastic points.

The imaginary identifications are themselves ferments of practical identifications or *mimetisms*. The stars guide our manners, gestures, poses, attitudes, ecstatic sighs ("It's fantastic!"), sincere regrets ("I'm sorry, Fred, I feel very friendly toward you, but I could never love you"), the way we light a cigarette, exhale the smoke, the way we lift a glass—casually or with significant sex appeal—the way we wave or tip our hat, the way we make roguish, profound, tragic faces, decline an invitation, accept a present, refuse or permit a kiss.

Many mimetisms focus on clothes. Even before 1914, when the French cinema ruled the world market, each new film "shown in a capital city immediately provoked numerous requests for similar costumes from elegant women."[1] Subsequently Hollywood stars have exerted their vestmental influence on the great mass of people. In 1930 the manufacturer Bernard Waldam had the idea of channeling the current by launching his magazines *Screen Stars Styles* and

Cinema Modes, and henceforth clothes inspired by successful films were standardized and distributed to a world market.

If the Parisian haute couture decides the length of next season's skirt and still holds a monopoly on fashion from season to season, the stars have posted themselves in the avant-garde of fashion's currents, modifying or breaking with the accepted notions of chic. In 1941 several great Hollywood actresses adopted masculine stuffs and styles—tweeds, shorts, tailored shirts—while male stars began to use materials and patterns hitherto considered feminine. A star is capable of overturning any dogma in the world of fashion. Naked under his shirt in *It Happened One Night*, Clark Gable caused such a decline in the sale of undershirts that knitwear manufacturers demanded the suppression of the scene.

The star, as an ideal, superior, and original archetype, is expected to determine fashions. Fashion permits the elite to differentiate itself from the common, hence its perpetual movement; and fashion permits the common to resemble the elite, hence its incessant diffusion.

The mimetisms of appropriations in principle are infinite when concerning objects similar to those the star is supposed to consume, use, or possess; they extend from sweaters to undershorts, from whiskey and soda to ice skates (of which the sale increased 150 percent after the first movies of Sonja Henie). Which is why the formidable system of modern advertising, tapping the current for its own mercantile ends, has increased and multiplied it. The star is always good advertising.

Furthermore, the star is not only a tutelary genius who guarantees the excellence of a product. In effect, she invites us to use *her* cigarettes, *her* favorite dentifrice—that is, to identify ourselves with her. She sells soaps, panty girdles, refrigerators, lottery tickets, novels, all of which she infuses with her virtues. The purchaser appropriates, consumes, and assimilates into his own personality a little of the star's body and soul.

Hence we can understand that the star's greatest effectiveness functions in relation to merchandise already infused with erotic magic. She is especially called upon to exalt beauty products and erogenous substances, modern equivalents of love potions (cosmetics, lotions, and so on).

More generally, nothing in our modern canon of the erotic does not undergo, in one fashion or another, the influence of the stars. They have helped to suppress the masculine costume inherited from British puritanism—the dark clothes of clergyman and sinner alike—in favor of bold, virile outfits (leather jackets, Italian sweaters) and brilliant colors. The feminine form has molded itself ever more closely in sweaters and slacks; has discovered new beaches of naked flesh.

The zones of erotic fixation of the human body, especially the hair, are henceforth under the star's spell. A hairdresser could write a history of the movies, starting with Mary Pickford's curls. Reciprocally, a scenarist could write a history of hairdressing. The fashion—and the term—*platinum blond* comes from Jean Harlow (*Hell's Angels*, 1930). In 1936 Greta Garbo's straight, smooth hairstyle spread over the United States. Then Norma Shearer's coiffure in *Romeo and Juliet*. The lock of hair falling over Veronica Lake's right eye had such a success that employers were said to have implored the star to wear her hair differently, since typists, reduced to monocular vision, were making twice as many mistakes. In France, after *The Eternal Return* innumerable white-haired Yseults à la Madeleine Sologne appeared in every town. Nor does the mimetic current spare the tonsorial system of the male stars, in which the successive coiffures of Marlon Brando and James Dean have enjoyed such structural triumphs. Beyond these particular imitations, it is the entire magic of the coiffure that has been supereroticized, greatly enlarging the enormous shampoo and hair dye industries.

Hollywood is even more obviously the source of the

modern makeup industry. The beauty treatments given the stars by Elizabeth Arden and Max Factor, the unguents and creams created for them, have been multiplied for all the faces in the world. These tubes and jars, these beauty creams, these cucumber milks, these egg yolks, these entire laboratories poured out on the dressing table of the humblest secretary are like a thousand alchemies borrowed from the stars in order to resemble them all the more closely. Chemistry and magic unite in the morning and evening mimetic rites: a new image, a Hollywood face, is created in front of the mirror.

And the lips! Joan Crawford's lips are superimposed on millions of mouths throughout the world. The natural shape of the lips disappears under a second, bloody, triumphant mouth, ceaselessly revarnished to provoke the mental kiss of every passerby.

The beauty industry, in its amazing scope, transmits and diffuses the canon modeled on the star standard. The female face has become a witch mask of seduction in the image of those of the screen. All the creams, paints, greases, ornaments, dresses, and undresses sustain one another in their united appeal to the heart and its gestures of love and desire. The gestures charged with eroticism, the gestures of smoking, drinking—the ritual and significant gestures of lovemaking—are the most directly patterned after those of the stars, as was revealed as far back as 1929 in Herbert Blumer's investigation.[2]

The star gives lessons in the techniques and exact rites of amorous communication, charming little pouts, keen smiles, romantic expressions, words inspired by moonlight ("How beautiful the moon is tonight"; "The night seems magical, darling, doesn't it?"), the style of confidence and confidences ("When I was a little girl I used to tell my doll . . ."), a way of murmuring "I love you," an ecstatic smile, rolling eyes, and, finally, the kiss.

The kiss in Hollywood films becomes identified with the

declaration of love. The latter, in forty films analyzed by Edgar Dale in 1930, is effected in 22 percent of the cases by an embrace, in 16 percent by a kiss, and in 40 percent by a kiss and an embrace.[3] In 142 films made in the years 1930–32 there were 741 kiss scenes. This Hollywood kiss obeys well-defined rules, for it is neither the chaste contact of two pairs of lips nor an overgluttonous suction, but a superior symbiosis in which spirituality and a carnal frisson reach a new harmonious balance. And millions of mouths repeat this kiss every day, every night—the first sacrament of modern love.

We do our best not only to resemble the star, but to make those we love resemble her as well. American parents, says Margaret Thorp, tortured their children for fifteen years by curling their hair like Shirley Temple's, making them drink the same milk or eat the same kind of oatmeal, as if they could thereby acquire the same talents for dancing and singing. The National Hairdressers and Cosmetologists Convention of 1939 rejoiced that "thanks to Shirley, beauty salons for children had appeared throughout the country."

In another sense the identification can be so intensely lived that it determines behavior in a decisive fashion: "In any annoying or aggravating situation I found myself wondering what Deanna would do" (letter of a nineteen-year-old girl).[4] This kind of identification can be exaggerated to the point of hysteria, as in the case of young Yvette S., who was afflicted with blindness after having seen Michèle Morgan in *La symphonie pastorale*.[5]

Thus the star is essentially a patron-model. The patron-model can be an inclusive archetype ("as beautiful as a movie star"; "I feel very 'Hollywood'") or a special case, each devotee imitating the star she thinks she most resembles ("My face is shaped just like Deanna Durbin's"; "I have Joan Crawford's looks"). The patron-model who determines the exterior appearance (clothes, makeup) can also give counsel concerning the soul's conduct and attitudes:

the star who gives "good advice" becomes a guardian angel and even identifies herself with the voice of conscience ("What would Deanna have done in my place?"). In every way, from every angle, the star is a patron and a model.

The process of identification with patron-models affects the problem of human personality itself. What is personality? Myth and reality both. Each of us has his own personality, but each of us lives the myth of his own personality. In other words, each of us fabricates an artificial personality that is, in a sense, the contrary of our real personality. Personality is generated by imitation as much as by creation. The personality is a mask, but a mask that allows us to make our voices heard, like the mask of the ancient theater. The star provides the image and the model of this mask, this disguise; we assimilate it into our character, integrate it with ourselves.

Thus the diversity, the multiplicity, the effectiveness of a thousand little mimetisms allow us to divine the stars' profound role in our lives, a role that is more readily explained if we consider ourselves in a genetic perspective of twentieth-century individuality. All individuality is the product of a dialectic of participations and affirmations of the self. The star releases a flux of such affirmations and participations, all imaginary.

These imaginary affirmations and participations can repress and inhibit the more practical kind, to the point of bringing about a schizophrenic personality type. As the British secretary of twenty-two who since childhood had devoted herself to the cult of the stars puts it, "And yet I have finished some really very pleasant friendships because of this intangible longing for something different: something based, I suppose, on my very early idea of love." The imaginary identifications can become so satisfactory that life itself is held in contempt. As in the case of the young girl discussed by Margaret Phillip: fascinated by the movies, she lived, entirely in her imagination, the life of a Japanese movie star, according each moment of her solitary existence to that of her heroine, even to the point of flagellating herself.[6]

But these imaginary participations and affirmations inspired by the stars also release concrete participations and affirmations. Directly or indirectly, the stars encourage participations in play (children's games), excursions, travels, and, above all, amorous participations.

The dialectic of imaginary and practical influences functions precisely where real human life is semi-imaginary and the imaginary life semi-real. At one extreme, this dialectic encourages a narcissistic withdrawal into the self; at the other it encourages an affirmation of the self, a will to live. In both senses it leads to personal salvation, either in the dream world or the world of waking, or in that world in which dream and daylight mingle in each other.

This salutary role illuminates the practical mimetisms that we have examined. All these imitations of elegant manners, of coiffure, of beauty, of seduction have the same purpose: to achieve success, to establish the self. All these imitators are expressing a profound need to affirm their own individuality. These triumphant red lips, the ardent smile of beauty itself, this need to love and be loved reveal that every woman wants to transform herself into a little idol, into a miniature star.

The star naturally plays the role of model. But she does not provide mimetism with merely the usages and rites of well-brought-up, rich, respected social types. *She incarnates a new elite. She proposes a new ethics of individuality, which is that of modern leisure.*

The ethics of leisure was born from the new needs of the twentieth century; it orients the affirmation of personality beyond the cursed zone of "piecework" to the exaltation of those activities that counterbalance and cast such servitude into oblivion. The star, like the sports champion, the mountain climber, the aviator, expresses the ideals of the ethics of leisure but, furthermore, provides these ideals with a concrete outlet by offering them the most exquisite, most entrancing, most individualistic, most immediately consumable fruit of leisure: love.

The star thus promotes the flowering of an ethics of love. She tends to identify—with extreme intimacy and extreme power—the affirmation of modern individuality with amorous participation. A love queen, she invites each of us to share the only royalty, the only divinity permitted today to even the humblest among us: to be loved. She urges us to live our "adventures" as well as to "live our lives"; she encourages us to struggle against time and age by seduction, the beauty of her lotions and her lips. The ethics of beauty, supported and protected at every step against the outrages of time, and the ethics of love, in which "the heart has no age" because it is "forever twenty," are two fundamental modern expressions of the ethics of individuality, which ultimately denies death and refuses to admit defeat.

The star's role is most effective evidently at the moment of the psychological and sociological hesitancy of adolescence, when the personality is still groping for its own limits. It is scarcely an exaggeration to say, with Seldes, that the movies are made for children and adolescents.

The great majority of the mimetisms that we have discussed here actually concern young people. It is the young who take movie heroes as the models on which to base their own individualities. It is the young who assimilate the imaginary star in order to lead themselves to real love. "I thought my girl would like a good imitation of Gable" (British boy, twenty-four years old).[7] The star provides not only information but *formation*, not only incitation but *initiation*. She reveals the forms of a caress, an embrace, the techniques of a kiss, develops the myth of miraculous and all-powerful love, inviting the reproduction of the sacred mystery on the altar of fatal, sublime, transcendent love. And from the imagined kiss to the kiss realized, from the new dream born of this kiss to its ultimate accomplishment, in a love progressively and effectively lived at subway entrances, Saturday-night dances, in open fields or a locked bedroom, the star's initiatory function is fulfilled.

Hence the manifold transferences that can take effect in the movie theater itself, where the adolescent finally takes his girl's hand, caresses it, and kisses it. Where, cheek to cheek, they live out their love in the love of the stars: "Watching a romantic film with a boyfriend, I let him kiss me" (twenty-two years old). "While watching one of those violent love scenes, a burning sensation runs through me, I want to do the things I see on the screen, and must admit that when I do them it's very pleasant."[8]

We quote an apprentice hairdresser, sixteen years old, to illustrate the process of transference from the star to every-day love:

> I always wanted to be an actress, and that was all I wanted. What's strange is that I have never really imitated an actress or an actor. I only wanted to know things about them, who they married. The only screen idol I ever fell in love with was Leslie Howard, but later I won a contest in which my idol gave away the prizes, and although he was charming, I realized he wasn't as nice as Tony, my poor boyfriend who had patiently waited until my aberration was over.[9]

The initiating function concludes when the adolescent liberates herself by transferring to her partner everything the star has inspired in her, including adoration. Of course the star can continue to excite and sustain partial mimetisms, she can survive in the world of the imagination like a great, floating dream, a beautiful impossibility that still leaves a few regrets within the secret heart. But her role as an initiating agent will be all the more effective if it has disappeared as soon as the transference is accomplished.

Nevertheless, the star's influence can persist after adolescence wherever the personality has weakly defined its interior frontiers between dream and reality—that is, more often in women than in men, and more often at intermediary social levels. Which is to say, ultimately, among women at intermediary social levels: white-collar workers; lower-middle-class housewives; dreaming, unfulfilled country girls. Which is why the star system has chiefly devoted itself to feminine requirements, feminine beauty, the fabrication of great courtesans.

The stars' influence is also extended beyond the cinema public by the intermediaries of the press, radio, television, and what we might call chain mimetisms. The star—particularly the Hollywood star—radiates over the whole world. She proposes and commercializes a familiarity with being, an experience of love, a knowledge of life. She assists in the worldwide diffusion of a concept of love, a whole culture of love, very particular to Western society. She increases the erotic emphasis of the human face. Movie stars have exalted, where it already existed, and introduced, where it was not yet known, the kiss on the mouth. The kiss is not only the key technique of lovemaking, not only the cinematic substitute for a coitus that censorship bars from the screen: it is the triumphant symbol of the role of the face and of the soul in the twentieth-century concept of love. The kiss keeps pace with the eroticism of the face, both equally unknown at primitive stages of society and still not practiced by certain civilizations today. The kiss is not only the discovery of a tactile voluptuousness. The kiss reanimates the unconscious myths that identify the soul with the breath emanating from the mouth; it thus symbolizes a communication or a symbiosis of souls. The kiss is not only the pimento that spices every Western film; it is the profound expression of a love complex that eroticizes the soul and mysticizes the body.

Hollywood movies distribute around the globe the products that thereafter function like ferments in the many preindustrial, non-middle-class, national cultures. What syncretisms will result? Can another culture, founded on other

requirements, a culture generated, say, by a socialist orientation, combat this influence? In what way? We cannot yet foresee the answers to such questions.

To sum up: the star intervenes and functions on every level of life, the imaginary level, the practical level, and especially on the level of the dialectic between the imaginary and the practical, that is, in the bacterial cultures of affective life where the personality elaborates and modifies itself. In order to understand this polymorphous action, we must appeal to the three fundamental effects of every spectacle: *catharsis*, *mimesis*, and, to employ a neologism, a *psychosis*.

Let us say, very roughly, that at the stage of childhood a film's effects have a cathartic-mimetic reciprocity. Such effects are expressed in games (play mimesis), and by these particular games the mimesis resolves itself into a catharsis. At the stage of adolescence, a socializing mimesis appears, which contributes to the formation of the adult personality. At this stage the stars' influence is most effective. Already the "psychotic" influence of the stars appears, which can result in complete withdrawal into the self and the characteristic Bovary neurosis; in this sense the stars contribute to the deepening of individual solitude. Actually, of course, the stars increase both solitude and participation, but these do not cancel each other out; they are the solitudes and the participations developed by the evolution of contemporary individuality.

It is ultimately in a complex manner, at once differentiated and convergent, that the star participates in the dialectic of the imaginary and the real, which forms and transforms modern man within the general evolution of civilization. Thus the stars, *patterns of culture* in the literal sense of the term, give shape to the total human process that has produced them.

The star is indeed a myth: not only a daydream but an idea-force. The characteristic of the myth is to insert itself or incarnate itself somehow within life. If the myth of the

stars incarnates itself so astonishingly within reality, it is because that myth is produced by that reality—that is, the human *history* of the twentieth century. But it is also because the human reality nourishes itself on the imaginary to the point of being semi-imaginary itself.

The stars live on our substance, and we on theirs. Ecto-plasmic secretions of our own being, they are immediately passed down the production lines of the great manufacturers who deploy them in galaxies stamped with the most distinguished trademarks. We drape ourselves naively enough in this immaterial tissue. But where is the star? Where is man? Where is the dream? We have looked for them on earth, and in the most intimate as well as the most contemporary regions of the human heart we have sought these coordinated doubles who, spread out under analysis, might subsequently permit us to read the map of the heavens themselves.

May the reader pardon us. Only here, at the point where we shall conclude, might such analyses be undertaken in which each star could be envisaged and contemplated in her irreplaceable individuality, her spell, her presence, her perfume. But we believe that before evoking Rita Hayworth, or Ava Gardner, or Gina Lollobrigida in all her particularity, it was necessary to reconnoiter the kingdom of the stars, to say where, in what country, Gina is the beautiful Roman . . .

Morin's Cinema Landmarks

1895	Birth of the movies.
1895–1908	Development of cinematic language, from Méliès to Griffith.
	Films have neither heroes nor stars.
1908	Film heroes appear: Nick Carter.
	Famous stage actors are introduced on film.
	The Assassination of the Duke de Guise.
1912–14	First great films: *Cabiria*.
	Vamps flourish in Danish cinema.
	Femmes fatales flourish in Italian cinema (the "divas," Lyda Borelli, Francesca Bertini, etc.).
	Mary Pickford becomes a star.
	Zukor founds Famous Players.
	The stars appear in cinema. The vamp acclimates herself to the United States (Theda Bara).
	First construction of studios in Hollywood.
1915	A new style of actor: Sessue Hayakawa in *The Cheat* (Cecil B. DeMille).
	Charlie Chaplin appears (Essanay series).
	The Birth of a Nation, first American superproduction (D. W. Griffith).
1916–18	Flowering of the American cinema. The western appears.

1918–26	Development of Swedish cinema: Victor Sjöström, *The Phantom Carriage*, 1920.
	Development of German cinema: Robert Wiene, *The Cabinet of Doctor Caligari*, 1920.
	The French avant-garde film: Abel Gance, *La roue*, 1923.
	Potemkin (Sergei Eisenstein), *The Mother* (V. I. Pudovkin): first masterpieces of the Soviet cinema (1926).
	Hollywood becomes the dominant center of world film production. Apogee of the star system: Rudolph Valentino, Douglas Fairbanks, Lon Chaney, John Gilbert, Wallace Reid, Mary Pickford, Gloria Swanson, Norma Talmadge, Clara Bow, Pola Negri, Greta Garbo.
1927	The first talking film: *The Jazz Singer* (Alan Crosland).
	Greta Garbo in *Flesh and the Devil* (Clarence Brown).
1929–30	The talkies become an art.
	Hallelujah (King Vidor).
	Sous les toits de Paris (René Clair).
1930	Marlene Dietrich in *The Blue Angel*.
1931–38	New stars are more intimate and "realistic": Irene Dunne in *Back Street* (J. M. Stahl), Clark Gable and Claudette Colbert in *It Happened One Night* (Frank Capra), Gary Cooper in *Mr. Deeds Goes to Town* (Frank Capra).
	In France, Préjean, Gabin, Annabella, Danielle Darrieux, etc.
1938–39	Michèle Morgan in *Port of Shadows* (Marcel Carné).
	Clark Gable and Vivien Leigh in *Gone with the Wind*.
1940	Charlie Chaplin in *The Great Dictator*.
1940–45	Jean Marais and Madeleine Sologne in *The Eternal Return* (Jean Delannoy).
	Humphrey Bogart in *The Maltese Falcon* (John Huston).
1946	Rita Hayworth in *Gilda* (Charles Vidor).

Ingrid Bergman in *Spellbound* (Alfred Hitchcock).

Shoe Shine (Vittorio De Sica) and *Paisà* (Roberto Rossellini), films without stars.

1947   Gérard Philipe and Micheline Presle in *Devil in the Flesh* (Claude Autant-Lara).

1948   Anna Magnani in *L'amore* (Rossellini).

La terra trema (Luchino Visconti) and *The Bicycle Thief* (de Sica), films without stars.

1949   Cécile Aubry and Michel Auclair in *Manon* (Henri-Georges Clouzot).

Silvana Mangano in *Bitter Rice* (Giuseppe De Santis).

Orson Welles in *The Third Man* (Carol Reed).

1950   Forgotten former stars become historical curiosities: Gloria Swanson in *Sunset Boulevard* (Billy Wilder).

1951   Ava Gardner in *Pandora and the Flying Dutchman* (Albert Lewin).

1952   Marilyn Monroe in *Niagara* (Henry Hathaway).

1953   CinemaScope.

Audrey Hepburn in *Roman Holiday* (William Wyler).

Alan Ladd in *Shane* (George Stevens).

1954   Grace Kelly in *To Catch a Thief* (Hitchcock).

1955   James Dean in *Rebel without a Cause* (Nicholas Ray) and *East of Eden* (Elia Kazan).

1956   Cult of James Dean.

Notes

This edition of *The Stars* attempts to complete, as much as possible, bibliographical information from the original publication. In-text citations have been moved to the endnotes, and a bibliography has been created.

Foreword

1. The 1972 edition of *Les Stars* also contains an appended essay on Ava Gardner, "the great mother goddess of the *De Rerum Natura*, who fantastically incarnates herself within the realist framework of the western film and explodes this realism with her mythic thrust" (my translation). As I note in my introduction to Morin's *The Cinema, or The Imaginary Man* (Minneapolis: University of Minnesota Press, 2005), this is one of Morin's most knowingly delirious essays.

2. To take just one example of contemporary work, anthropologist Lila Abu-Lughod's treatment of Egyptian born-again Islamic female stars' relation to their audience promises to be very interesting in this respect. See Lila Abu-Lughod, *Dramas of Nationhood: The Politics of Television in Egypt* (Chicago: University of Chicago Press, 2004).

Genesis and Metamorphosis of the Stars

1. Balázs, *The Theory of Film*, 288.
2. Stephen Watts, *Film Technique*, 83.
3. Thorp, *America at the Movies*, 76.

Gods and Goddesses

1. Gentilhomme, *Comment devenir vedette de cinéma*.

2. Jean Marais, preface in ibid.

3. Bilinsky, "Costume," 54.

4. Gary Cooper, Clark Gable, and Errol Flynn, approaching their sixties, are not old, but real men. Their wrinkles come from interesting experiences, not dilapidation. These rough trappers of movie space are more virile than ever.

5. Margaret Thorp cites the disagreeable effect of Irene Dunne's drunkenness in *Joy of Living* on her admirers. *America at the Movies*, 64.

6. See Rosten, *Hollywood*, 45–46.

7. Arlaud, *Cinéma bouffe*, 163.

8. Rosten, *Hollywood*, 182.

9. Ibid., 124.

10. Ibid.

11. Possessed by her own myth, the star imposes it on the film universe of which she is the product. Stars demand or refuse roles in the name of their own image. Pierre-Richard Wilm wanted to make only films in which he would be victorious in love; Gabin, before 1939, demanded his own death in every film he made.

12. See Rosten, *Hollywood*, 60.

The Stellar Liturgy

1. Quoted in Thorp, *America at the Movies*, 100–101.

2. The following quotations are from Mayer, *British Cinemas and Their Audiences*.

3. Quoted in Curt Riess, *Hollywood inconnu*, 105.

4. Roy, *Hollywood en pantoufles*, 80.

5. *Motion Picture Herald*, October 5, 1940.

6. Quoted in Riess, *Hollywood inconnu*, 105.

7. Mayer, *Sociology of Film*.

8. Dekeukeleire, *Le cinéma et la pensée*, 50.

9. See T. E. Sullenger, "Modern Youth and the Movies," *School and Society*, 1930–32, 459–61, an investigation made among 3,295 high school students; Gallup Poll published by *Time* magazine, July 21, 1941; results of the Bernstein Children's Film Questionnaire, London, 1947; investigation of the Motion Picture Research

Bureau in Handel, *Hollywood Looks at Its Audience*, 147, in which 65 percent of the subjects preferred stars of their own sex.

10. The following survey results are from Handel, *Hollywood Looks at Its Audience*, 142.

11. Both quoted in Mayer, *British Cinemas and Their Audiences*.

12. This and the following two quotations, ibid.

13. Clair, *Adams*, 50.

The Chaplin Mystery

1. Piceni, "Guirlande pour Charlot," *Le Rouge et le Noir*.

The Case of James Dean

1. Similarly, it is quite recently that adolescence has been studied by psychology as such (Debesse).

2. George Stevens tells that it was James Dean himself who asked to interpret this role: "It's a part for me, Mr. Stevens."

3. François Truffaut, in *Arts*, September 26, 1956.

Star Merchandise

1. Bachlin, *Histoire économique du cinéma*, 171.

The Star and the Actor

1. Manvell, *Film*, 78.

2. Pudovkin, *Film Acting*, 150–52.

3. Feuillère, in *Le cinéma par ceux qui le font*, ed. D. Marion, 161.

4. Page, "Le chef opérateur du son," 222–23.

5. Sadoul, *Le cinéma*, 127.

6. Critics such as André Bazin have emphasized the increased importance of the director, but from the point of view of *the art of direction*.

7. Moussinac, *Naissance du cinéma*.

8. Sadoul, *Le cinéma*.

9. Hampton, *A History of the Movies*.

10. Pudovkin, *Film Acting*, 150.

11. Lionel Barrymore, in *La technique du film*.

12. Max Ophuls, in *Cahiers du Cinéma* 54 (Christmas 1955): 7.

13. Quoted in *Hollywood Spectator*, November 1931, 8.

14. Dullin, "Human Emotion," *Art Cinématographique*.

15. Supervielle, "*Cinéma*," 182.

16. Francis, "Reflections on Cinematic Interpretation," 391.

17. Eisenstein quoted in Altman, "Cinéma sovietique," 126–27.

18. Dovzhenko quoted in ibid., 123.

19. Eisenstein quoted in ibid., 127.

20. Balázs, *The Theory of Film*, 79.

21. Dougherty, "Close-up and Long Shots," 26.

The Star and Us

1. Gael Faim, in L'Herbier, 449–50.

2. Blumer, *Movies and Conduct*.

3. Dale, *The Content of Motion Pictures*.

4. Quoted in Mayer, *Sociology of Film*, 180.

5. See *Annales d'Occulistique* 180 (1947): 104–6.

6. Phillip, *The Education of the Emotions*.

7. Quoted in Mayer, *British Cinemas and Their Audiences*.

8. Quoted in Blumer, *Movies and Conduct*.

9. Quoted in Mayer, *British Cinemas and Their Audiences*.

Bibliography

Altman, G. "Cinéma sovietique." *Art Cinématographique* 8 (1931).

Arlaud, R.-M. *Cinéma bouffe: Le cinéma et ses gens*. Paris: Jacques Melot, 1945.

Bachlin, Peter. *Histoire économique du cinéma*. Paris: Le Nouvelle Édition. 1947.

Balázs, Béla. *Theory of the Film: Character and Growth of a New Art*, translated by E. Bone. New York: Dover, 1970.

Bilinsky, B. "Le costume." *Art Cinématographique* 6 (1929): 25–56.

Blumer, Herbert. *Movies and Conduct*. New York: Arno, 1970.

Dale, Edgar. *The Content of Motion Pictures*. New York: Macmillan, 1935.

Dekeukeleire, Charles. *Le cinéma et la pensée: Le cinéma art-clef de l'analyse du monde moderne*. Paris: Éditions Lumière, 1947.

Dougherty, Kathryn. "Close-up and Long Shots." *Photoplay*, December 1932.

Francis, Eve. "Reflections on Cinematic Interpretation." In *Anthologie du cinéma*, edited by Marcel Lapierre. Paris: Bernard Grasset, 1948.

Gentilhomme, Guy. *Comment devenir vedette de cinéma*. Paris: Éditions de l'Hermite, 1950.

Hampton, Benjamin E. *A History of the Movies*. New York: Covich-Friede, 1931.

Handel, Leo A. *Hollywood Looks at Its Audience: A Report of Film Audience Research*. Urbana: University of Illinois Press, 1950.

L'Herbier, Marcel. *Intelligence du cinématographe*. Paris: Corréa, 1946.

Manvell, Roger. *Film*. New York: Penguin, 1946.

Marion, D., ed. *Le cinéma par ceux qui le font*. Paris: Fayard, 1949.

Mayer, J. P. *British Cinemas and Their Audiences: Sociological Studies*. London: Denis Dobson, 1948.

————. *Sociology of Film: Studies and Documents*. London: Faber, 1946.

Moussinac, Léon. *Naissance du cinéma*. Paris: J. Povolozky, 1925.

Page, L. "Le chef opérateur du son." In *Le cinéma par ceux qui le font*, edited by D. Marion, 208–24. Paris: Fayard, 1949.

Pudovkin, V. I. *Film Technique and Film Acting*. New York: Grove, 1970.

Rosten, Leo. *Hollywood: The Movie Colony, the Movie Makers*. New York: Arno, 1970.

Roy, Jean. *Hollywood en pantoufles*. Paris: Éditions du Blé Qui Lève, 1947.

Sadoul, Georges. *Le cinéma, son art, sa technique, son économie*. Paris: Bibliothèque Française, 1948.

Supervielle, Jules. "Cinéma." *Cahiers du Mois* 17–18 (1925).

La technique du film. Paris: Payot, 1939.

Thorp, Margaret. *America at the Movies*. New Haven, CT: Yale University Press, 1939.

Edgar Morin, emeritus researcher at the Centre national de recherche scientifique, is one of France's leading contemporary philosophers. He has written on scientific method, philosophical anthropology, social theory, popular culture, and contemporary life, and his oeuvre combines the humanities and the social sciences in an ongoing dialogue that grasps the complexity of the real. Among his most important works are *La méthode* (1977–2004) and *Chronique d'un été* (*Chronicle of a Summer*, 1960), a landmark documentary film made in collaboration with Jean Rouch. He is also the author of *The Cinema, or The Imaginary Man* (Minnesota, 2005).

Richard Howard has translated many books of French criticism, including works by Roland Barthes, Michel Foucault, and Tzvetan Todorov. His most recent literary translations include *Absinthe: A Novel*, by Christophe Bataille, and Stendhal's *The Charterhouse of Parma*. A poet and critic, he teaches at the School of the Arts at Columbia University.

Lorraine Mortimer is senior lecturer in sociology and anthropology at La Trobe University in Melbourne, Australia. She translated Morin's *The Cinema, or The Imaginary Man*.